the Glycemic Load Diet

A POWERFUL NEW PROGRAM FOR LOSING WEIGHT AND REVERSING INSULIN RESISTANCE

ROB THOMPSON, M.D.

New York Chicago San Francisco Lisbon London Madrid Mexico City
Milan New Delhi San Juan Seoul Singapore Sydney Toronto

The McGraw·Hill Companies

Library of Congress Cataloging-in-Publication Data

Thompson, Rob, 1945–
    The glycemic-load diet : a powerful new program for losing weight and
reversing insulin resistance / by Rob Thompson.
        p.   cm.
    Includes bibliographical references and index.
    ISBN 0-07-146269-4
    1. Reducing diets.   2. Glycemic index.   3. Insulin resistance.
    4. Weight loss.   I. Title.

RM222.2.T4847   2006
613.2'83—dc22   2005032432

20 21 22 23 24 25   QFR/QFR   1 5

ISBN 978-0-07-146269-3
MHID   0-07-146269-4

McGraw-Hill books are available at special quantity discounts to use as premiums and
sales promotions or for use in corporate training programs. To contact a representative,
please visit the Contact Us pages at www.mhprofessional.com.

The information contained in this book is intended to provide helpful and informative
material on the subject addressed. It is not intended to serve as a replacement for
professional medical advice. Any use of the information in this book is at the reader's
discretion. The author and publisher disclaim any and all liability arising directly and
indirectly from the use or application of any information contained in this book.

To Kathy, Maggie, John, and "Nan"

Contents

Part 3

STRATEGIES TO BALANCE YOUR METABOLISM AND STAY ON TRACK

Acknowledgments

I AM INDEBTED to my agent, Elizabeth Frost-Knappman, for encouraging me to write this book and shepherding it through its early stages. Natasha Graf, my editor at McGraw-Hill, was immensely helpful, bringing her considerable talents to bear on guiding me through the development and organization of the manuscript.

Molly Siple, M.S., R.D., provided exactly the recipe-writing touch I was seeking. Ms. Siple is nutrition editor at *Natural Health* magazine, chef extraordinaire, and author of several acclaimed cookbooks, including *Low-Cholesterol Cookbook for Dummies* (John Wiley and Sons, 2004), *Healing Foods for Dummies* (IDG Books, 1999), and *Recipes for Change: Nutrition/Cookbook on Foods for Menopause* (Dutton, 1996). She has taught at the Southern California Cordon Bleu School of Culinary Arts and continues to lecture and write articles on cooking and nutrition.

I would like to thank my longtime friend Lean Carroll for carefully reading and editing the manuscript and patiently sharing her thoughts with me. I am also indebted to my office staff, Nadine Warner, Lisa Gierlinski, and Charlene Brown, for so often going beyond the call of duty to make my life enjoyable. Most of all, I would like to thank my wife, Kathy, certainly for her editing skills but especially for her unwavering patience, encouragement, and support.

Introduction

WHEN I STARTED practicing medicine twenty-five years ago, I followed the party line. I recommended calorie counting and low-fat diets for weight loss and was usually disappointed by the results. People just kept gaining weight. Then, in the 1990s, some of my patients started ignoring warnings about fat and cholesterol and going on low-carb diets. The results were astonishing. Folks who had been unsuccessful at losing weight for years started shedding pounds more easily than they thought possible even as they ate generous amounts of rich food. Remarkably, their blood cholesterol and sugar levels looked better than ever. It was as if they had stopped ingesting a toxin that had been poisoning them for years. I became convinced that the low-carbohydrate approach had tremendous potential for helping people lose weight and regain their health. Indeed, as additional research came out, the medical establishment, mired in low-fat orthodoxy for decades, has come around to thinking the same way.

But just when medical science is focusing more attention on carbohydrates, the public's interest in low-carb diets is waning. People rushed to try the Atkins diet—a radical low-carb regimen popularized in the 1970s—and the South Beach diet, a sort of second-generation Atkins diet, but the programs didn't work the way they hoped. People lost weight but usually gained it back. Although these diets allowed plenty of rich food, they created irresistible food cravings. People just couldn't continue them for long. Disillusionment set in, and the low-carb craze began to die down.

In recent years, billions of dollars have been spent researching human body chemistry. Medical science knows much more about carbohydrate metabolism now than it did when the low-carb movement began:

- Food scientists have developed a way of measuring the metabolic effects of different carbohydrates, called the *glycemic index*. This concept, only in its infancy when the low-carb movement began, has evolved into a powerful model, the *glycemic load*. This new way of looking at carbohydrates radically changes the low-carb approach to losing weight. It is the key to a natural weight-loss-promoting eating style that is satisfying and easy enough to follow for life.
- Scientists now know that most overweight people have a genetically influenced metabolic disorder called *insulin resistance* that makes them susceptible to weight gain from eating carbohydrates with high glycemic loads. Researchers have pinpointed the foods and behavior patterns that bring out this condition and can now target treatment toward relieving it.
- Recently, physiologists have discovered the metabolic quirk that causes insulin resistance. It's a disorder of the body's *slow-twitch* muscle fibers. What's exciting is that exercising these muscle fibers creates much less fatigue than exercising others.

These and other new concepts can help you harness the weight-loss power of carbohydrate modification and slow-twitch muscle activation with a lifestyle that's much easier to follow than previous weight-loss regimens. It really is possible to lose weight without "dieting," in the usual sense of the word, or engaging in strenuous exercise.

Over the years that I've worked with people trying to lose weight, I have developed a sense of what people are capable of.

I am convinced that willpower is not a prerequisite for success and, in fact, can be a liability. When it comes to losing weight, we all have limited supplies of energy and discipline. What's critical is finding the right strategy, and the key is *knowledge*. If you come to understand the physiological disturbances that caused you to gain weight, you will know exactly what you need to do to lose it. Indeed, once you see the light, I think you'll find that shedding pounds and keeping them off for good are much easier than you thought.

Part 1

Insulin Resistance: A Hormonal Imbalance, Not a Character Defect

1

Understanding Why You Gained Weight

t's enough to drive you crazy. You're constantly battling your weight while others seem to stay thin effortlessly. They don't exercise, they eat anything they want, but they don't get fat. The perplexing thing about the obesity epidemic—and this has been true of other scourges throughout history—is that some people are more vulnerable than others. They suffer from the harmful effects of our modern lifestyle, while others seem to be immune. Overeating and lack of exercise are not the whole story.

But for years, people thought that being overweight was a matter of choice. Just as some folks played golf or did crossword puzzles for enjoyment, others got their kicks from eating. Doctors knew of certain hormonal disturbances that could make people gain weight, but they thought these were unusual. Most overweight people just chose to be the way they were.

Of course, who in their right mind would choose to be fat? If it came to a decision between being overweight or getting hit by a truck, some people would probably opt for the truck. Almost everyone would agree: obesity is unattractive, cumbersome, and unhealthy.

Being overweight, then, suggested you were either weak-willed or had some kind of psychological problem. However, when psychologists got around to studying overweight people systematically, they came up empty-handed. It turns out that overweight people are psychologically no different from thin folks. They have some bad habits, but no more than anybody else. They get a little depressed, but who wouldn't be? One thing is certain: they aren't weak-willed. Obese people often show remarkable self-discipline in other aspects of their lives. After all, 65 percent of Americans are overweight. Do all of these people have some kind of character defect? Of course not.

It's Not a Matter of Willpower

Do you remember when you were a kid and you tried to see how long you could hold your breath? It was easy at first, but after a minute or so, you developed a different mind-set. Lack of oxygen triggered chemical reflexes that told you in no uncertain terms you needed to breathe. Certainly, the need for oxygen is more urgent than the need for food, but the principle is the same. If you reduce your caloric intake, changes in your body chemistry stimulate powerful hunger-driving reflexes that overrule lesser concerns like how good you look. When those instincts say "eat," unless you have unusual willpower, you eat. You can postpone it for a while—and you have some control over the *kinds* of foods you eat—but if you try to defy the urge, you usually come away the loser.

The reason self-deprivation rarely works for losing weight is that it defies deeply rooted survival instincts. Consider this: Your body burns about 1.2 million calories a year. If your weight depended on your consciously regulating the amount you eat, misjudging by 2 percent (that's about two bites of a potato a day) would add or take off forty-two pounds in ten years. Who can fine-tune their eating that much? Your body can't afford to rely on your whims. It has its own mechanisms for balancing calorie intake with energy output.

Just as a lack of willpower didn't make you gain weight, simply willing yourself to eat less is unlikely to result in lasting weight loss. You might think you can dial down your calorie consumption at will, and maybe you can for a while. But let's face it: if you're like most people, you'll eventually return to your old ways.

A Matter of Hormones

In recent years, scientists who study body chemistry have discovered several hormones that regulate body weight. Here are a few examples:

- Your thyroid gland makes a hormone called *thyroxin*, which helps regulate how fast your body burns calories.
- Your stomach secretes *ghrelin* to stimulate your appetite when your stomach is empty.
- Your intestines produce *peptide YY* to curb your appetite when your intestine has enough food to work on.
- Your fat cells secrete *leptin* to reduce your appetite when your fat stores have been replenished.

Those are only some of the hormones known to control weight, and scientists are still discovering new ones. The point is this: powerful chemical reflexes regulate the balance between the calories you take in and the rate you burn them off. Body weight is *not* simply a matter of choice.

The hormone systems that regulate body weight evolved over millions of years during times when hunger was a constant threat. Although these mechanisms helped keep fat accumulation in check, their main purpose was to prevent starvation. Of course, our diet and activity patterns have changed a lot since the Stone Age, but our body chemistries work the same. When our weight-regulating systems sense we're not getting enough to eat, hunger-stimulating hormones arouse powerful cravings, and energy-regulating hormones reduce the rate at which our bodies burn calories. The desire to eat dominates our thoughts, and our bodies do everything they can to replenish fat.

So the reason you're overweight is not that you lack willpower. It's because something upset the systems that match your caloric intake with your energy expenditure. Certainly, choices *were* involved. You influenced the form those calories took—whether they were carbohydrates, fats, or protein—but your body's weight-regulating mechanisms determined how much food you needed to quell your hunger. You can't ignore those instincts. Mustering up the discipline to starve yourself is not the answer. You need an approach that doesn't rely on willpower.

But if you have such little control over how much you eat, how can you lose weight? It's easier than you think, but you just can't do it by a frontal assault on deeply rooted survival instincts.

There are dozens of ways to lose weight. You can cut fats, cut carbs, count calories, fast, go on an exercise kick, or have your stomach stapled. But if a particular problem—say a hormonal imbalance, a lifestyle quirk, or a certain kind of food—caused you to gain weight, does it make sense to starve yourself without trying to correct the conditions that caused the problem in the first place? If you don't fix what's wrong, whatever caused you to gain weight is bound to come back and haunt you.

Unlocking the Mystery of Obesity

In recent years, billions of dollars have been spent on researching human metabolism, and indeed, medical science has made major breakthroughs in solving the mystery of obesity. Although these advances have been obscured by the usual controversy, junk science, and diet hype that surround the issue of weight loss, old ways of thinking are being turned upside down. Scientists now have a clearer idea of why people's weight-regulating mechanisms fall out of kilter and what can be done to put them back in balance. Here is the picture that is emerging.

If you're like most overweight people, three conditions converged to cause you to accumulate excess fat:

1. You inherited a common genetic quirk that affects a type of muscle fiber in your body called a *slow-twitch fiber*, making these muscles resistant to the effects of *insulin*, a hormone needed to metabolize the sugar glucose.
2. Lack of regular activation of your slow-twitch fibers causes them to spend too much time in a metabolically

dormant state in which they don't respond normally to insulin, a condition called *insulin resistance*.

3. The insensitivity of your muscles to insulin makes you vulnerable to the harmful effects of dietary *starch*, the main ingredient of "white" carbohydrates like bread, potatoes, and rice. Starch releases more glucose into your bloodstream and does it faster than any other kind of food.

If your muscles are resistant to insulin and you consume quantities of starch typical of our modern diet, your pancreas gland has to make *five or six times* the normal amount of insulin to handle the glucose in your blood. And that's the problem. Insulin is a powerful obesity-promoting hormone—scientists call it the "feasting hormone." It triggers overeating and encourages your body to store calories as fat. Try as you will, you can't keep the pounds off.

There's another problem with starch: instead of traversing the full twenty-two feet of your digestive tract as other foods do, it short-circuits into your bloodstream in the first foot or two. It never reaches the last part of your intestine, where certain appetite-suppressing hormones come from. Even though starch is chock-full of calories, a few hours after eating it, you're hungry again.

Sleuthing the Hormonal Culprit: Syndrome X

Doctors have known for years that certain medical conditions can throw people's weight-regulating mechanisms out of kilter. The best known of these conditions is *hypothyroidism*, an underactive thyroid gland. Many folks wish they had this condition because it's so easy to correct with pills. However, most people's weight problems are not caused by thyroid trouble.

Although doctors have known for years of conditions that cause obesity in *some* people, until recently they couldn't pinpoint what caused *most* people's weight gain. Whatever it was, though, it was apparent that it was extremely common, the modern lifestyle aggravated it, and it got worse with age. Then scientists got a clue from doctors who took care of heart patients. In the 1980s, clinicians began to notice that patients who had heart attacks had an unusually high incidence of the following physical characteristics and laboratory findings:

- *Visceral adiposity*, a tendency to accumulate fat in the abdomen
- High blood levels of a type of fat called *triglyceride*
- Low blood levels of *HDL*, a protective kind of cholesterol particle also called "good cholesterol"
- Mildly elevated blood pressure
- Borderline high blood glucose levels

When several of these findings occurred in the same individual, it raised the risk of blood vessel blockages even when blood cholesterol levels were normal. Not knowing what caused this phenomenon, doctors called it *syndrome X* or the *metabolic syndrome*.

Solving the Mystery: Insulin Resistance

Recently, researchers solved the mystery of syndrome X. It's caused by *insulin resistance*. This discovery was to turn the world of nutrition upside down and invalidate much of what doctors previously believed about diet, obesity, and heart disease. It also explained why excessive dietary starch and physical inactivity make some people gain weight but not others.

Insulin resistance isn't exactly a disease—it's a variation in the way people's bodies process carbohydrates, foods your body breaks down to glucose. About 22 percent of the American population can't handle the starch and sugar in their diets without producing excessive insulin. Although these folks usually have a genetic propensity to insulin resistance, having the tendency doesn't necessarily cause the condition. People who are hereditarily predisposed can go their entire lives without manifesting it. Something else—something in their activity and eating patterns—has to bring it on.

Insulin resistance is basically a *muscle* problem. Your muscles are the main users of glucose, and insulin regulates their consumption. Exercise increases your muscles' responsiveness to insulin, so they take up more glucose. Inactivity decreases their sensitivity, so they take up less. While the lack of physical activity that characterizes the typical modern lifestyle causes some degree of insulin resistance in everybody, it renders the muscles of genetically prone individuals *particularly* insensitive to insulin.

Although lack of physical activity brings on insulin resistance, this wouldn't be such a problem if we ate only meat and raw vegetation, as our prehistoric ancestors did. The body doesn't need much insulin to handle those foods. Meat contains virtually no glucose, and the glucose in fresh fruit and vegetables trickles into our bloodstreams slowly, requiring only small amounts of insulin. The only foods in our diet that call for large amounts of insulin are refined carbohydrates. Insulin resistance becomes a problem only when we consume more starch and sugar than our bodies can handle.

There's another important factor that brings on insulin resistance: being overweight itself. It's a vicious cycle. Weight gain worsens insulin resistance, and insulin resistance, in turn, promotes more weight gain. Even if you weren't insulin resistant to begin with, if you're overweight, you're more insulin resistant now than you were before. Insulin resistance *locks* you into being overweight.

The Thrifty-Gene Hypothesis

Why are so many of us genetically prone to such a troublesome condition as obesity? One benefit of being overweight is that you can withstand starvation better than thinner folks can. In ancient times, when humans regularly went long periods without food, the ability to store up calories as fat was an advantage. Because this trait increased the chances of survival during famine, more and more humans passed it on to the next generation. Biologists call this explanation for why we get fat the "thrifty-gene hypothesis."

Did the tendency to store excess fat predispose our ancestors to diabetes and heart disease? Undoubtedly, it did, but in prehistoric times, people rarely lived long enough to develop such problems. In the Stone Age, the average life span was less than thirty years. Also, people's diet and activity patterns helped protect them from these conditions.

How Insulin Resistance Affects Your Health

Excessive demands for insulin, high blood triglyceride levels, and wide fluctuations of blood glucose levels typical of unchecked insulin resistance cause myriad health problems, including the following:

- **Type 2 diabetes:** If insulin production can't keep up with demand, glucose levels begin to rise, causing the condition called *type 2 diabetes*. Uncontrolled diabetes literally sugarcoats tissues and can eventually lead to eye, kidney, and blood vessel damage.
- **Islet cell burnout:** The islet cells of the pancreas, which secrete insulin, also make a substance called *amylin*. When they secrete excessive amounts of insulin they also produce excessive amylin. High concentrations of amylin turn into an insoluble sludge called *amyloid* that damages the very cells that secrete it. Biopsies of the pancreases of patients with type 2 diabetes often show replacement of insulin-secreting cells by amyloid.
- **Hypoglycemia (low blood sugar):** One of the earliest signs of insulin resistance is what's commonly called "low blood sugar." It might seem strange that a condition that leads to high blood sugar could cause low blood sugar, but when insulin-resistant individuals go three or four hours without eating, they often experience weakness, poor concentration, and a strong craving for food, all of which are promptly relieved by

eating. Actually, the term "low blood sugar" is a misnomer. When the pancreas has to make large amounts of insulin, it often overshoots, causing glucose levels to fall too fast. This triggers a surge of another hormone, *adrenaline*, which stops glucose from falling. It's the adrenaline—not low blood glucose—that causes the shakiness and poor concentration typical of hypoglycemia. Adrenaline highs and lows typically occur several times a day, causing quirky eating patterns, frayed nerves, and end-of-the-day fatigue.

- **Heart and blood vessel disease:** When your body gets more glucose than it can handle, your liver turns the excess to fat globules, which travel through your bloodstream to your fat deposits in the form of triglyceride. Although triglyceride doesn't damage arteries directly, high concentrations reduce blood levels of "good cholesterol," HDL, which raises the risk of blood vessel disease even when bad cholesterol levels are normal. (I talk about this more in Chapter 11.)

- **Menstrual difficulties:** In women, insulin resistance sometimes brings on *polycystic ovary syndrome (PCOS)*, which causes irregular periods, ovarian cysts, abnormal hair growth, and acne. PCOS is the leading cause of female infertility in the United States, affecting approximately 6 percent of women. It can be treated with a low-starch diet, exercise, and insulin-sensitizing medication.

- **Sleep apnea:** Accumulation of fat in the abdomen and neck typical of insulin resistance interferes with breathing during sleep. This causes excessive snoring and aggravates *sleep apnea*, a form of erratic breathing that robs sleep of its restfulness.

Making the Diagnosis

Although doctors recognized that many of their patients had insulin resistance, they had no idea how common it was until researchers tested large segments of the population. According to a recent government study, 22 percent of the American population has insulin resistance—44 percent of those older than fifty years. Among overweight individuals, the incidence is 85 percent. The bottom line is this: if you're overweight, you probably have insulin resistance.

Measuring insulin resistance directly is a tedious laboratory procedure usually done only in research centers. However, doctors found they could accurately surmise its presence by looking for signs of syndrome X. Here are the criteria, defined by the National Cholesterol Education Program, for diagnosing it. If you have any three of the following five characteristics, you probably have insulin resistance:

1. **A tendency to accumulate fat in the abdomen:** abdominal girth measured at your navel of thirty-eight inches or more if you're a male or thirty-four inches if you're a female, or a waist measurement more than 95 percent of your hip circumference measured around your buttocks if you're a male, 85 percent if you're a female
2. **High blood triglyceride level:** a triglyceride level greater than 150
3. **Low blood level of good cholesterol:** an HDL level below 40 if you are male or 50 if you are female
4. **Borderline or high blood pressure:** systolic blood pressure greater than 130 or diastolic blood pressure greater than 85
5. **Borderline or high blood glucose:** fasting blood glucose level greater than 110

Super X'ers

Viewed from behind, you could hardly tell Henry was overweight. He had narrow hips and little fat on his arms or legs. However, in profile you could see that he had a potbelly. His abdomen extended several inches beyond his belt. His girth was forty-two inches. His triglyceride level was 280.

When Henry reduced his starch intake and started walking regularly, he lost weight. Impressed at how easy it was, he began testing himself to see how much rich food he could get away with eating. He was amazed to find that he could consume generous amounts of fatty foods—even more than he was naturally inclined to eat—yet continue to lose weight.

I often encounter patients who have especially flagrant signs of syndrome X—abdominal girth more than forty-two inches for males or thirty-eight inches for females and triglyceride levels greater than 225. I call such folks Super X'ers. It's gratifying to work with these individuals because they usually respond dramatically to measures that relieve insulin resistance.

For Super X'ers, eliminating carbohydrates is like taking away a toxin from people who have been poisoning themselves. As long as they avoid starch, they often seem to be immune to gaining weight from eating fat.

How You Can Reverse Insulin Resistance

The good news is that if you have insulin resistance, you don't have to put up with it. Few conditions in medicine are so easy to treat. Of course, you can't change your genes. However, you *can* stop the blood glucose surges that trigger excessive insulin secretion, and you *can* restore your slow-twitch muscles' sensitivity to insulin. You do it by cutting out a handful of bland and unexciting foods and engaging in some physical activity that even couch potatoes don't mind doing. If you do both of those things, your insulin levels will drop like a rock, your metabolism will fall back into balance, and probably, without trying to cut calories or engaging in strenuous exercise, you will steadily lose weight.

Is this hard to do? Put it this way: there's no easier way to shed pounds. For one thing, starch is essentially tasteless. It releases a few aromatic chemicals during chewing and a small fraction breaks down to glucose in your mouth that you *can* taste. However, most of it ends up in your stomach without your tasting it. When you eliminate starch, you're essentially only removing flavorless paste. Most of the satisfying tastes and textures in the food you eat stay. In addition, starch contains no important vitamins or minerals. This is important because deficiencies of vital nutrients create irresistible food cravings. Getting rid of refined carbohydrates only makes you healthier. No creature ever died for lack of starch.

As for activating your slow-twitch muscle fibers, if you ascribe to the no-pain, no-gain philosophy of exercise, you might find what I'm going to tell you hard to believe, but there are muscles in your body that require virtually no effort to exercise. A good example is your diaphragm, the main breathing muscle beneath your rib cage. It doesn't take much effort to breathe, does it? These kinds of muscles are powered by slow-twitch fibers, which, as it turns out, are the ones that determine your body's sensitivity to insulin. (I cover this in more detail in Chapter 8.) In other words, the muscles you need to activate to relieve insulin resistance are precisely the ones that require the least effort to use. Even folks who dislike exercise can do it and actually enjoy it.

The combination of removing the starch from your diet and activating your slow-twitch muscle fibers is also the *simplest* way to lose weight. Although I have included many delicious low-starch recipes in this book, there is actually no need for special food preparation. You can go to the same restaurants as before, eat alongside everybody else, and attract no attention. You only need to avoid a handful of foods, which you can quickly learn to recognize.

You Can Start Today

At your next meal, hold off eating any bread, potatoes, or rice until you finish everything else, and then, if you must, have about a quarter of what you usually eat. *Do not deprive yourself of food.* Make up for eating less starch by helping yourself to more of everything else. This is not a calorie-cutting diet. It's a way of reducing the amount of insulin your body has to make.

If in addition to reducing your intake of those "white foods" you walk thirty minutes every other day, after a few days, your body chemistry will function much differently than it did before. Your pancreas will make a fraction of the insulin it was producing, your blood sugar will stop fluctuating wildly, and fat globules will disappear from your blood. You will have removed the driving force behind your weight gain.

You might also notice that you feel better. Highs and lows of blood glucose cause your body to make excessive amounts of adrenaline, which jars your nerves and leaves you feeling burned out and exhausted. Smoothing out these fluctuations makes you feel calmer and gives you more energy later in the day.

Believing in What You're Doing

It is possible to lose weight by doing either of those things—eliminating foods that cause glucose surges or increasing your muscles' sensitivity to insulin—but the secret is to do both. The two approaches *potentiate* one another—that is, one makes the other more effective. Eliminating blood glucose surges improves your muscles' sensitivity to insulin, and improving your muscles' sensitivity to insulin stabilizes blood glucose levels.

Although the changes you need to make to relieve insulin resistance are as small as they can possibly be and still produce weight loss, they are changes nonetheless, and they need to be permanent. This is not a fad diet meant to be started and stopped when you have reached a goal. To ingrain new eating habits and activity patterns, you need to believe in what you're doing and know how to do it. In the next few chapters, I'm going to show you the science behind the principles I have outlined here. Once you understand what made you gain weight, you'll see clearly what you need to do. You'll learn what the easiest, most effective way is to stop your body from overproducing insulin. If instead of trying to starve yourself you concentrate on correcting what caused you to gain weight, you'll be astonished at how easy it is to shed pounds and keep them off for good.

2

Starch Toxicity:
How Our Staples
Turned Out to Be Toxins

One thing is for sure, if your weight has been creeping up lately, you're not alone. A lot of us have the same problem. How did so many of us get this way?

To gain weight, you have to take in more calories than you burn off. Otherwise, your body would defy the laws of thermodynamics. The question is not *whether* you consumed more calories than you burned off but *why* you consumed more calories than you burned off. Your body has weight-regulating mechanisms that are supposed to balance food intake with energy expenditure. What's throwing those systems out of kilter?

You hear a lot these days about toxins in the food chain—things like mercury, PCBs, and iodine. The alleged culprit is usually a chemical introduced into the environment by humans and found to be harmful to laboratory animals in large doses. The media sound the alarm, people fuss about it for a while, and then the hysteria dies down. No one seems to get sick from these things. As a doctor, I've personally never seen any illness I could relate to mercury, PCB, or iodine toxicity. It makes interesting news, but the amounts of these pollutants in our food are usually much too small to make us sick.

However, I do see patients suffering from the effects of another toxin every day. It's a mixture of two chemicals, *amylase* and *amylopectin*, that people introduced into their food only recently in the span of human existence. But unlike the toxins you read about in the newspapers, this one exists in our food in, frankly, toxic concentrations. Although its effects are subtle, sometimes taking years to do its damage, it often leads to progressive disability, disease, and death. Where are we getting this toxin? We make a point of adding it to nearly every meal we eat. It's the main ingredient of bread, potatoes, and rice and is more commonly known as *starch*.

Bread, Potatoes, and Rice: How "Natural" Are They?

Starch is, in fact, the same tasteless paste laundries use for stiffening shirt collars. The word starch comes from the Old English word *sterchen*, "to stiffen," which is what it does to your arteries. Most of us don't think of starch as a toxin because the foods that contain it are so familiar to us. We've been eating bread, potatoes, and rice all our lives, as have our parents and grandparents. Indeed, many people can get away with eating large amounts of starch without harmful effects because they are genetically resistant to its harmful effects or have certain activity patterns that protect them. However, for those of us who are susceptible—which includes about 40 percent of the population—starch toxicity is a menacing reality. Consumption of amounts common in our modern diet can lead to serious problems like diabetes and heart disease—but not before causing years of unsightly, frustrating obesity.

When you're young, your body can handle a lot of starch. Your pancreas makes plenty of insulin, and your tissues respond very well to it. However, as you age—especially if you have a genetic predisposition to insulin resistance—the way your body metabolizes glucose slowly changes. Your pancreas continues to make plenty of insulin, but your body begins losing its responsiveness to it. As a result, your pancreas has to make increasing amounts of insulin to keep your blood glucose levels down. As time passes, your body's ability to produce insulin begins to lag. If the pancreas can't secrete enough insulin to overcome insulin resistance, glucose starts backing up in the bloodstream, the condition we call *diabetes*.

The tissues that line blood vessels are particularly vulnerable to high blood glucose levels. Diabetes eventually leads to blood-vessel disease, the most common cause of death and disability in the industrialized world. However, diabetes is only the late stage of starch toxicity. Profound body chemistry disturbances precede diabetes by decades, causing quirky appetite regulation and imbalances between good and bad cholesterol that promote cholesterol buildup in arteries. The most frustrating problem, though, is a tendency to accumulate excess body fat.

Starch Poisoning: The Price of Civilization

How did the foods we rely on most to prevent hunger—the so-called staples like wheat, potatoes, and rice—end up causing so much trouble? For millions of years, humans roamed the earth, hunting game and gathering natural vegetation for food. Starch was not a major part of their diet. They consumed it only in minute quantities locked in the protective husks of seeds that were not particularly appealing to eat.

In nature, starch provides a concentrated source of energy for seeds to sprout. The seeds of grasses that are native to regions with long, hot dry seasons and short, temperate wet seasons are especially high in starch, which jump-starts these plants so they can mature quickly during short growing seasons. Impermeable husks protect the seeds from the sun and predators during the dry season.

Around ten thousand years ago—very recently in the span of human existence—people living in the eastern Mediterranean region and South Asia, where wheat and rice grew naturally, figured out how to extract the starchy cores of the seeds from their protective husks by grinding them between rocks. They used these kernels to stave off starvation when meat and fresh vegetation were scarce. For the first time, humans discovered a plentiful source of calories for which they didn't have to compete with other predators and that they could store for months.

Later our ancestors found that by adding water and heating these kernels, they could make them more palatable. As time passed, they discovered more ways to make starch taste better. They added fat to flour to make it moist, leavened it with yeast to lighten it, and added sugar to sweeten it. Because high-starch foods have to be processed or "refined" before they can be eaten, they have come to be called *refined* carbohydrates.

The cultivation of wheat in the West, rice in Asia, and corn in the New World was a boon to humankind. These staples pro-vided—and continue to provide—an efficient means of prevent-ing starvation. Of all the foods humans eat, refined carbohydrates supply by far the most calories with the least investment of land, labor, and capital.

Not only did the domestication of wheat, rice, and corn change the human diet, but it also transformed civilization. The ability to stockpile food supplies freed humans from having to forage constantly. This encouraged cooperation, division of labor, and eventually formation of governmental structures. Along with government and spare manpower came armies of conquest. Even-tually, the eastern Mediterranean and South Asian regions gave rise to the dominant civilizations of the world, and reliance on starchy staples spread to most societies on earth.

A Monumental Change in Body Chemistry

The cultivation of refined carbohydrates represented a major change in the human body's chemical environment. Prehistoric humans ate only small amounts of starch entangled in fiber and encapsulated in impervious husks. It takes hours for the diges-tive tract to process such foods. It was a shock to the human metabolism when, instead of the occasional granule of starch, people began consuming cupfuls at every meal in concentrated, rapidly digestible form.

Your body handles refined carbohydrates differently from other kinds of foods. As soon as starch hits your stomach, it breaks down to glucose, which short-circuits directly into your bloodstream without traveling more than a few inches down your intestinal tract. Within minutes, your blood glucose levels shoot up to heights never experienced by your prehistoric ancestors.

If genetic changes were needed to handle this abrupt change in digestive physiology, the human race has not had enough time to evolve them. Genetic adaptation requires millions of years, but starchy staples have been around for only about ten thousand— a mere tick of the evolutionary clock. It isn't surprising that the shift to refined carbohydrates that has occurred in the last few thousand years has had a profound effect on human health.

The Two Faces of Starch Toxicity

Excessive starch consumption manifests itself in two ways, depending on whether there is sufficient intake of other foods. In underdeveloped countries where populations rely heavily on starchy staples for survival, refined flour, rice, and potatoes have supplanted other sources of nutrition, many of which are vital to good health. Because starch provides little in the way of vitamins, minerals, or protein, deficiencies of these nutrients are rampant in these areas. In parts of Africa and Asia that rely heavily on starchy staples, as much as 40 percent of the population suffers from iron-poor blood caused by lack of meat and iron-containing vegetables. Iron deficiency is so widespread in some countries that it measurably affects their economies. Another major health problem in poor countries is *kwashiorkor*, a disease of protein deficiency. This condition weakens the immune system and causes children to die of otherwise minor illnesses like measles and chicken pox. In addition, many children in these regions suffer from *rickets*, a disease of calcium deficiency that causes weakening and bending of bones. These conditions are practically unheard of in areas with adequate supplies of meat and dairy products.

Excessive consumption of refined carbohydrates causes a different set of problems in developed countries. In these parts of the world, people can choose from a wide variety of foods, and vitamin, mineral, and protein deficiencies are rare. But while most inhabitants of industrialized nations aren't dependent on starch for survival, they still eat large amounts of it. The problem in these countries is not the crowding out of other foods by starch but rather the toxic effects of starch itself. Excessive amounts of refined carbohydrates have caused epidemics of obesity and diabetes.

Why Do We Eat So Much Starch?

Economics drive our dependence on starch. Bread, potatoes, and rice are cheap. People can eat their fill without spending a lot of money. Not only is starch economical for consumers, it's cheap for food producers, and sometimes they can obtain patents on their processing techniques so other firms can't compete with them. This allows manufacturers to sell their products at high profit margins. The potential for large profits encourages producers to think up ever more imaginative ways to prepare and market starch, and large price markups over production costs allow revenue for advertising. Consequently, firms that manufacture brand-name processed foods, like crackers, chips, and breakfast cereals, advertise heavily. In contrast, producers of foods in their natural state can't obtain patents on their products. Without the ability to exclude competition, suppliers of fresh fruit, vegetables, meat, and dairy products have to maintain competitive prices. The only way they can make a profit is by keeping their overhead down. Consequently, they don't advertise much. You rarely see television ads for fresh produce.

As a rule, when others are paying for the ingredients of the food you eat, their economic incentive is to feed you starch. That's why restaurants are happy to see you fill up on bread, potatoes, and rice. The profit margin on a McDonald's hamburger is razor thin. Fast-food restaurants make most of their money selling french fries and soft drinks.

The Obesity Epidemic: How America Got Fat

In 1962, 13 percent of the American population was obese (defined as being thirty pounds overweight or more), and that percentage had remained stable for decades. Then, around 1970, the numbers suddenly started rising. By 1998, the proportion of obese Americans more than doubled to 31 percent, and the incidence of diabetes, which is often brought on by excessive weight gain, rose sixfold. What caused the obesity rate to suddenly shoot up like this?

You'll hear many explanations for why so many people are overweight these days. Proponents of various theories usually cite some evidence to support their opinions, but the data are often flawed. It's hard to study people's diets. You can't put humans in pens, the way you can with laboratory animals, and control what they eat. In a sense, though, we all live in a sort of pen—the one defined by our national borders. The U.S. Department of Agriculture keeps close tabs on the types of foods Americans eat, and the National Health and Nutrition Examination Survey carefully tracks people's height and weight. If you combine these two sources of data, you can gain some compelling insights as to why we are gaining weight.

In the 1950s and 1960s, Americans reveled in their ability to eat fresh farm food, including eggs, meat, and dairy products. For the first time in history, mass agricultural production, refrigeration, and rapid transportation made these goods available and affordable for most citizens. Americans remembered harder times during the Great Depression, when people suffered from iron-deficiency anemia and rickets caused by lack of adequate nutrition. To be able to enjoy fresh produce, which prevented such conditions, was a privilege.

Then, around 1970, something came along that chilled America's ardor for eggs, meat, and dairy products. Government agencies and medical organizations, concerned about the rising incidence of heart disease, started recommending low-fat, low-cholesterol diets—not just for people prone to artery disease but for everybody. The theory was that reducing the cholesterol in food would reduce cholesterol in people's blood and prevent heart attacks. This public health effort coincided with a rise in popularity of vegetarianism and a period of rampant inflation of meat and dairy product prices. The result was an abrupt shift in eating patterns away from eggs, red meat, and dairy food. Table 2.1

Table 2.1 Annual Consumption of Red Meat, Eggs, and Milk, 1970 Versus 1997

| | Consumption per Person | | |
| | | | Change, |
Type of Food	1970	1997	1970 to 1997
Red meat	132 lb.	111 lb.	Down 16%
Eggs	309 eggs	239 eggs	Down 23%
Milk fat (equivalent in whole milk)	114 qt.	55 qt.	Down 52%

Source: U.S. Department of Agriculture National Nutrient Database

shows how consumption of these foods has changed since 1970. Clearly, Americans did exactly what government agencies and doctors told them to do: they cut down on fat- and cholesterol-containing foods. We are now eating 16 percent less red meat, 23 percent fewer eggs, and 52 percent less milk fat per person than we did thirty years ago.

If you eat less of one kind of food, you're bound to eat more of another. Indeed, Americans are now eating more *carbohydrates*—plant-based foods. The biggest change in the American diet in the last thirty years has been a dramatic increase in consumption of *refined* carbohydrates: flour, rice, and potatoes. As you can see from Table 2.2, we are eating 48 percent more flour,

Table 2.2 Annual Consumption of Flour, Rice, and Potatoes, 1970 Versus 1997

| | Consumption per Person | | |
| | | | Change, |
Type of Food	1970	1997	1970 to 1997
Flour	135 lb.	200 lb.	Up 48%
Rice	7 lb.	20 lb.	Up 186%
Frozen potato products (mainly french fries)	13 lb.	30 lb.	Up 131%

Source: U.S. Department of Agriculture National Nutrient Database

186 percent more rice, and 131 percent more frozen potatoes, mainly french fries, than we did in 1970.

The Wheat-Obesity Link

America's largest source of starch by far is wheat. The graph in Figure 2.1 compares the average wheat consumption per person over the last forty years with the percentage of the population that is thirty pounds or more overweight. You can see that as soon as wheat consumption started rising in the 1970s, the obesity rate did the same. The message is clear: the more wheat Americans eat, the fatter they get.

What About Sugar?

Another carbohydrate we are eating more of is sugar. We Americans are consuming 26 percent more sugar per person than we did before 1970. But we're not eating it in the form of candy;

Figure 2.1 Obesity Rate Versus Annual Wheat Consumption per Person (1961–2000)

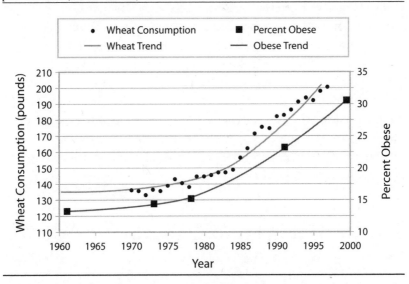

Source: National Center for Health Statistics Third National Health and Nutrition Examination Survey and U.S. Department of Agriculture National Nutrient Database

candy consumption has remained stable over the past thirty years. Kids are consuming it in soft drinks, and adults are eating it in flour products like rolls, doughnuts, cookies, and cakes.

The starch in flour is essentially flavorless; you need to doctor it up to make it taste good. Sugar, in contrast, is overwhelmingly sweet; you have to dilute it to make it palatable. However, if you mix the two, you can give starch more flavor and tone down the sweetness of the sugar. Americans are consuming more sugar because they're eating more starch and drinking more soft drinks.

The Big "Fat" Lie

What about our supposed nemesis, fat? Government agencies, medical organizations, and vegetarian groups have been trying to convince us for years that we're gaining weight because we're eating too much fat, but that notion is so far off base you wonder if someone's putting us on. The truth is, we're eating considerably less fat and cholesterol than we did before the obesity epidemic began. Indeed, researchers have found that as people gain weight, they eat *less* fat and more carbohydrate. Clearly, dietary fat is not what's causing our weight problems.

Even though fast-food restaurants provide, on average, only 12 percent of America's caloric intake, they are frequently blamed for making folks fat. The reason given is that these places serve up too much "fatty food." But the next time you see a super-size meal in McDonald's or Burger King, ask yourself how much of what you are looking at is meat and dairy product, and how much is bun, french fries, and soft drink—that is, how much is fat, and how much is starch and sugar? Fast food isn't so much fatty as it is starchy and sugary.

Too Much Starch, Not Enough Exercise, or Both?

My grandmother, who lived on a farm, baked huge trays of cinnamon rolls every week. She kept her pantry stocked with fresh homemade bread. She boiled big pots of potatoes and served them mashed for dinner and fried for breakfast. Her icebox was filled with eggs, meat, and dairy products at all times. Her family could eat as much rich food as they wanted whenever they wanted. Talk about convenience foods—they didn't even have to drive to a fast-food restaurant. Why didn't *they* get fat?

Clearly, there's more to our obesity problems than the food we eat, be it starchy *or* fatty. The other side of the weight gain equation is the lack of physical activity that characterizes our modern lifestyle. My grandparents and their children didn't get fat because they did several hours of physical work every day. Indeed, researchers who study the effects of lifestyle on obesity find a much closer correlation with physical activity than with eating patterns.

Statistics show that the more time people spend commuting to work in automobiles, the more likely they are to be overweight. A while back, I saw a photograph in the *Seattle Times* taken in 1915 of a group of businessmen in downtown Seattle, and it struck me that they were all slim. I wondered what they did differently from us. They were wearing business suits, so I doubted they did physical work all day. The only difference I could think of from the businesspeople of today was that they probably walked to work; in those days, most Seattleites lived a mile or two from downtown. Not long afterward, I gave up my downtown parking place, left my car at home, and started walking to work.

Exercise does more than just burn off calories while you are doing it. It revs up your metabolism, activates hormonal systems, and increases your body's sensitivity to insulin for days afterward. When you exercise, you literally burn more calories while you sleep. Scientists have found that the higher the level of physical activity, the more precisely the body's weight-regulating mechanisms work. In other words, when you exercise, your body more accurately matches the calories you take in with the energy you burn off.

Nevertheless, although lack of exercise set the stage for Americans to gain weight, it doesn't explain why the obesity rate suddenly started rising thirty years ago. Activity levels had been declining for years. The largest reductions occurred in the first half of the century when Americans stopped doing farmwork and started driving cars, but before 1970 the obesity rate was half of what it is now and had remained stable for decades.

If we did as much physical work and walked as much as our ancestors, there would probably be no obesity epidemic. But what has changed the most in the past three decades has not been our exercise habits. It's been our diet. We're eating less fat but *much* more starch. The skyrocketing obesity rate of the last thirty years correlates precisely with a dramatic increase in our consumption of refined carbohydrates.

Starch toxicity isn't so different from other epidemics that have decimated human populations over the centuries, and it isn't the only disease to be wrongly blamed on character shortcomings. Humans conquered the scourges of the past only when they abandoned the notion that character defects caused them and began looking for medical causes. The obesity epidemic will be halted only when we stop focusing on personal shortcomings and begin addressing the metabolic disturbances that cause excessive fat accumulation, including our biologically unnatural dependence on refined carbohydrates.

3

Understanding What Makes
Bad Carbs Bad

He wasn't the first to discover it, but he was probably the most persistent. In the 1960s, New York cardiologist Dr. Robert C. Atkins found that when his overweight patients cut out plant-based foods—fruits, vegetables, grains, and sugar—many of them lost weight, even while eating generous amounts of rich, fatty foods. Remarkably, they seemed to be able to shed pounds without *trying* to cut calories.

Encouraged by these observations, Atkins devised a weight-loss diet for his patients that eliminated all carbohydrates. The only ones he allowed were green leafy vegetables in limited quantities. The results were impressive. Many of his patients experienced dramatic weight loss even while consuming large amounts of foods strictly forbidden by other diets, including red meat, cheese, and butter. In his book *Dr. Atkins' Diet Revolution*, published in 1971, dieters found a way to lose weight while continuing to eat many of their favorite foods—again, *without trying to cut calories.*

Unfortunately, Atkins's timing couldn't have been worse. Researchers had recently discovered links between high blood cholesterol and heart disease. In those days, nutritionists took the adage "you are what you eat" literally. They thought people had high blood cholesterol simply because they ate too much cholesterol, and got fat simply because they ate too much fat. Because most of the cholesterol and fat in the American diet came from animal products, they figured the best way to lower cholesterol and lose weight was to cut out eggs, red meat, and dairy products. This advice also resonated with people's vegetarian and animal rights beliefs. Not only was such a diet better for you, it was kinder to animals. A low-fat, low-cholesterol diet *high* in carbohydrates seemed to be the way to go.

Atkins's recommendation to eat fewer carbohydrates and more meat and dairy products soon became heresy. He was actually called before a congressional committee to defend his views and was publicly derided. It seemed for a while that his detractors had won. At the urging of the government and the medical community, and despite lack of proof of effectiveness, America started moving toward a lower-fat, lower-cholesterol, higher-carbohydrate diet.

The Weight-Loss Power of Low-Carb Eating

Atkins knew that the old saying "you are what you eat" is misleading. When it comes to fat, cholesterol, and carbohydrates, you really *aren't* what you eat. Your body can quickly transform carbohydrates to fat and fat to carbohydrates. People can get just as fat eating carbs as they can eating fat. In fact, unlike fat, carbohydrates stimulate your pancreas to secrete insulin, a hormone notorious for causing weight gain.

As a heart specialist, Atkins also knew that reducing *dietary* cholesterol didn't lower *blood* cholesterol much. Your body makes its own cholesterol—about three times as much as you eat. If you reduce the amount of cholesterol in your diet, your liver just makes more. The level of cholesterol in your blood is determined not by how much cholesterol you eat but by how efficient your system is at getting rid of it, and that's mainly a matter of genetics. When it comes to cholesterol, who your parents are is much more important than what you eat.

The more experience Atkins gained, the more certain he became that a low-carb, liberalized-fat diet was safe for most people and more effective for losing weight than low-fat diets. In 1991, more than twenty years after his first book, he published *Dr. Atkins' New Diet Revolution*. The enormous impact this book made was as much a matter of timing as it was content. Twenty years of low-fat, low-cholesterol advice seemed only to have made Americans fatter. People were desperate to lose weight and ready to try anything: diet pills, jaw wiring, stomach surgery—whatever did the job. When some folks ignored concerns about cholesterol and turned to the Atkins diet, they again discovered that it worked. People who had failed to lose weight with other programs often succeeded with the Atkins diet. They told their friends and, for the second time, Atkins's radical low-carb, high-fat diet became popular.

The resurrection of the Atkins diet in the 1990s was a grass-roots movement. The medical community had nothing to do with it. For the most part, doctors and nutritionists were chagrined. Mired in low-fat, low-cholesterol orthodoxy, they feared an epidemic of high blood cholesterol, but the scourge never materialized. One difference between the 1970s and the 1990s was that in the nineties, doctors routinely checked cholesterol levels and were better able to detect heart disease. They didn't find any tendency for low-carb diets to cause heart problems or even raise cholesterol. When their patients lost weight, they just seemed healthier for it.

In the late 1990s, researchers finally put the low-carb, liberalized-fat diet to the test, comparing it head-to-head with traditional low-fat, calorie-restricted diets. They found that Atkins was right after all; low-carb diets were more effective than low-fat diets. People lost more weight and, in most cases, their blood cholesterol levels improved. Best of all, they didn't have to go hungry. They could eat until they were satisfied and still shed pounds. Atkins was vindicated. Sadly, he died in an accident a month before the nation's most reputable medical journal, the *New England Journal of Medicine*, published the results of those studies.

Powerful but Not Sustainable

If you're overweight and do what Atkins recommended—cut out virtually all carbohydrates, including fruit, vegetables, grains, and sweets—you'll see dramatic things happen. You'll lose weight while consuming an amazingly rich diet. The level of fat in your blood (triglyceride) will plummet, your blood glucose and insulin levels will fall, and your good cholesterol level will rise. If you're typical, your bad cholesterol level won't change much or will fall slightly.

People who try the Atkins diet are often astonished at how fast the pounds melt away. I've seen patients lose weight so fast they thought something was wrong with them. Although I don't advocate such rapid weight loss, when I see such dramatic responses it's apparent to me that there's more to cutting carbs than reducing calories. It's as if people who have been inadvertently poisoning themselves for years discover the toxin and stop ingesting it. There's no question, carbohydrate restriction is a powerful weapon for losing weight.

Nevertheless, while it might be easier to shed pounds with a low-carb diet than with a low-fat approach, most folks who go on the Atkins diet fail to lose weight permanently. The problem is that they can't stick with the diet. Fruits and vegetables are full of vitamins, minerals, and fiber that are essential to good health. When people try to remove these nutrients from their diets, their bodies fight back, and they begin craving the missing foods. People also miss sweets, not necessarily to satisfy hunger, but just for the pleasure of tasting them. Eventually, their cravings for the forbidden foods overcome their motivation to continue, and they go back to their old ways. The choice of foods allowed by the Atkins diet and its more recent counterpart, the South Beach diet, is too narrow for most people to tolerate for long.

Because people can't stay on such diets for long, the low-carb craze eventually died down. But just as the public was becoming disillusioned, nutritional scientists were discovering ways that people could benefit from the weight-loss power of carbohydrate restriction without the diet-wrecking narrowness of these diets.

To appreciate how you can enjoy satisfying amounts of a much wider variety of foods and still lose weight, you need to understand the differences between rapidly digested and slowly digested carbohydrates.

Why Some Carbs Are Different from Others

As you learned in Chapter 2, it isn't *all* carbs that are making Americans obese; it's the refined ones, mainly wheat products, potatoes, rice, and sugar. What exactly is it about these foods that makes people gain weight? Let's go back to basic nutrition for a minute.

There are three distinct kinds of food: fat, protein, and carbohydrates. Each has its own building block. Fat is composed of *fatty acids*, protein of *amino acids*, and carbohydrates of *glucose*. Most of the fat in our diet comes from the fatty parts of meat, dairy products, and oily vegetables like nuts and olives. We get protein from eggs, dairy products, the lean parts of meat, and certain rich vegetables, including nuts and beans. Carbohydrates are plant products like fruits, vegetables, grains, potatoes, and sugar.

Before any of these foods can pass through the walls of your intestine into your bloodstream, your digestive tract has to sever the bonds that hold their molecules together and turn them back into their original building blocks. As food inches its way down your intestine, your digestive juices break down fat to fatty acids, protein to amino acids, and carbohydrate to glucose, the forms in which they enter your bloodstream.

Refined Carbohydrates Cause "Glucose Shocks"

Considering that all carbohydrates eventually break down to glucose, what difference does it make whether they're in the form of fruit, vegetables, starch, or sugar when you eat them? Until recently, nutritionists made no distinction—a carb was a carb. However, it turns out there's a big difference in the way various carbohydrates affect your body, and that difference is the key to understanding why refined carbohydrates make peo-

ple fat. It's also the key to losing weight without depriving yourself of satisfying amounts of good, healthful food.

The glucose molecules in carbohydrates are linked together
end to end like railroad cars. It's the job of your digestive system
to unhitch them so they can pass into your bloodstream. But
Mother Nature doesn't give up her bounty easily. The glucose
molecules of natural carbohydrates—whole fruits and vegetables—bond tightly to one another and intertwine with indigestible fiber and cellulose. It takes time for your digestive juices
to unhitch them and free them up. The glucose in these kinds of
carbohydrates trickles into your system slowly, over the course of
several hours.

However, it's a different story for starchy carbohydrates like
bread, potatoes, and rice. The bonds that hold their molecules
together are much weaker and easily severed by digestive juices,
and there's no indigestible fiber or cellulose to get in the way. As
soon as refined carbohydrates hit your digestive tract, their glucose molecules come unhitched and, within minutes, without having to travel more than a foot or two down your intestines, enter
your bloodstream. Instead of slowly leaching into your system, as
glucose in fresh fruit and vegetables does, the glucose in starch
rushes in all at once. Within minutes, your blood glucose shoots
up to levels never experienced by your prehistoric ancestors.
These "glucose shocks" are foreign to the way human digestive
systems worked for millions of years before starch came on the
scene. It's not surprising that refined carbohydrates wreak havoc
on the hormones that regulate body weight.

How Glucose Shocks Make You Gain Weight

Your pancreas secretes whatever amount of insulin it takes to
keep your blood glucose levels in a safe range. That's easy to do
when you eat the kind of food cave dwellers lived on—meat and
fresh vegetation. Your pancreas has to make only enough insulin
to handle small amounts of glucose that seep into your bloodstream over hours. However, when you eat refined carbs, large
amounts of glucose entering your bloodstream all at once forces

your pancreas to secrete large amounts of insulin. This is especially true if you have insulin resistance, in which case your pancreas has to secrete as much as six times more insulin than normal to get the job done. Over time, repeated glucose shocks can exhaust your pancreas and cause diabetes. Excessive insulin secretion has another important consequence: it encourages your body to store calories as fat.

Another problem with refined carbs is that they only travel a foot or two down your intestinal tract before they short-circuit into your bloodstream. They never get to the last part of your digestive tract, where certain appetite-suppressing hormones are produced. Normally, these substances act as messengers to let your brain know your intestines have received enough food so you'll stop eating, but starch doesn't get far enough down your digestive tract to trigger them.

Another peculiar quality of starch is that you actually don't taste much of it. A small fraction of it turns to glucose in your mouth, which you can taste, but most of it passes into your stomach without interacting with your taste buds. After it reaches your stomach, however, it immediately breaks down to glucose. This strange digestive pattern encourages weight gain. Sugar that you can taste causes less weight gain than sugar you can't. For example, scientists have found that glucose infused through tubes placed into the stomach has less of an appetite-satisfying effect than glucose taken by mouth.

All of these attributes of starch promote overeating and fat accumulation. In one research study, subjects who were fed starchy breakfasts and lunches consumed an astonishing 80 percent more calories in the afternoon and evening than subjects fed omelets, fruits, and vegetables. The bottom line is that refined carbohydrates are unnatural foods that behave unnaturally in our bodies. It's not surprising that the more of these "bad carbs" we eat, the fatter we get. The reason low-carb diets cause weight loss is not that they restrict carbohydrates in general. In fact, the more fruits and vegetables people consume, the *less* likely they are to be overweight. Low-carb diets work because they eliminate refined carbohydrates.

Moving Beyond Atkins

Atkins was on the right track. His diet eliminated refined carbohydrates. The problem was, it restricted too many other foods. Most people just can't go very long without fruits, vegetables, and a few sweets. However, Atkins was a man with a point to prove. After being called a charlatan in the 1970s, he was intent on proving that cutting carbs and continuing to eat fat and cholesterol could produce weight loss without raising blood cholesterol levels. His radical low-carb, high-fat diet convinced the world that he was right, but his advice never changed much. His diet was essentially the same in the 1990s as it was when he first recommended it in the 1960s.

It's been more than thirty years since Atkins published his first book. Although junk science, diet hype, and academic turf battles have obscured the progress that has been made, medical science knows much more about metabolism and nutrition now than it did then:

- Ten years ago, doctors didn't know about insulin resistance. Correcting this condition is the key to successful weight loss. Now that scientists have pinpointed the genetic flaw that causes insulin resistance, it's possible to target diet, exercise, and even medications toward relieving it.
- Nutritionists now know that only a few carbs trigger excessive insulin secretion. Many of the foods the Atkins diet forbids—including fruits, vegetables, milk, and even sweets—can actually help you lose weight. You only need to avoid a handful of bad carbs.
- Scientists have discovered that rapid weight loss triggers metabolic reactions that thwart further weight loss. Now you can take measures to counteract this diet-wrecking problem.
- Scientists have gained a much clearer understanding of what people need to do to keep their arteries healthy. With the right strategy, you can lose weight at the same time you lower your risk of heart and artery disease.

Thanks to these and other new discoveries about nutrition and metabolism, it is now possible to harness the weight loss power of low-carb dieting with a healthier, more enjoyable lifestyle that even people not endowed with unusual willpower can follow for life. The secret is in understanding something called the glycemic load and discovering how to activate your slow-twitch muscles, both of which you'll learn about in the next section of this book.

Part 2

The Glycemic-Load Diet and Slow-Twitch Muscle Activation Plan

4

Lightening Your Glycemic Load: The Key to Easy Weight Loss

The reason most diets fail is simply that people can't stick with them. Low-fat diets are especially hard to follow. People crave the richness of fat and quickly either fall off the wagon or try to satisfy their hunger by eating too much starch and sugar. Low-carb diets are easier to follow but often make the mistake of restricting too many foods. Currently popular low-carb diets limit fruits, vegetables, dairy products, and sweets and usually can't resist throwing in some low-cholesterol advice. All these restrictions inevitably lead to food cravings and diet failure, and most important, they divert attention from the real culprits: foods that raise blood insulin levels. As you learned in Chapter 3, the starch in refined carbohydrates causes your blood glucose to shoot up to levels never experienced by your prehistoric ancestors. These "glucose shocks" trigger excessive insulin secretion, which promotes fat accumulation.

Understanding Glycemic Indexes

It's difficult to predict whether a particular food will cause a glucose shock simply by measuring its carbohydrate content. Some carbs break down to glucose faster and raise insulin levels more than others do. Food scientists have learned that the best way to tell how high blood glucose goes after eating a food is to give a standardized amount to human subjects and measure their blood glucose levels afterward. Nutritionists now rate foods according to their *glycemic indexes*, the amount a food raises blood glucose compared with a benchmark—usually white bread. An apple, for example, has a glycemic index of 52, which means that a given amount of carbohydrate in apple raises blood glucose levels 52 percent as much as the same amount of carbohydrate in white bread.

Why Glycemic Indexes Are Misleading

The discovery that some carbs raise blood glucose levels more than others do was good news for low-carb dieters. They didn't have to avoid all carbohydrates, only ones with high glycemic indexes. Soon, popular diet books, such as *The South Beach Diet* and *The Glycemic Index Diet*, published lists of glycemic indexes to help low-carb dieters avoid glucose shocks. However, while these lists increased awareness of differences among carbs, they also created misconceptions that have kept the low-carb eating style from realizing its potential. To see how misleading these measurements can be, look at the glycemic indexes of the following foods:

Food	Glycemic Index
Tomatoes	23
Spaghetti	64
Carrots	68
White bread	100
Bagel	103

If you keep in mind that foods rated less than 55 are considered "low" on the glycemic index scale, you would conclude, correctly, that you don't have to worry as much about tomatoes as you do bagels, even though both are carbohydrates. However, notice that carrots, which you probably thought were good for you, have a higher glycemic index than spaghetti, a notoriously starchy food. That doesn't sound right, does it?

The Devil in the Details: Serving Size

It's important to understand that glycemic indexes are raw laboratory measurements. In fact, the researchers who developed these listings warned against using them *without correcting for the amounts people typically eat.* That may seem like a mundane technicality, but it makes a world of difference in the way you need to eat to avoid glucose shocks. Here's why glycemic indexes, which are not adjusted for serving size, are so misleading.

To measure the glycemic index of a food, scientists have to feed volunteers enough of it to provide fifty grams of carbohydrate *available for absorption into the bloodstream.* However, the amount of available carbohydrate in various plant-based foods varies tremendously. For example, because carrots contain so much water and *unavailable* carbohydrate in the form of indigestible fiber, to provide fifty grams of available carbohydrate, researchers had to feed each subject seven full-size carrots. In contrast, to provide fifty grams of available carbohydrate in spaghetti, they only had to feed subjects a cupful. Of course, most people don't eat seven carrots in one sitting, but they often eat a cupful of spaghetti or more. Glycemic indexes are misleading because the amounts researchers have to feed subjects to get these measurements bear little resemblance to the amounts people typically eat. The glycemic indexes of many fruits and vegetables, like carrots, turn out to be as high as many starchy carbohydrates, like spaghetti.

Missing Out on Good Carbs, Not Recognizing the Bad

The failure of popular diet books to correct glycemic indexes for serving size caused a lot of people to deprive themselves of healthful foods they didn't need to avoid. Research studies consistently show that the more fruits and vegetables people eat, the *less* obesity, diabetes, and heart disease they have. The fiber in fruits and vegetables prevents glucose shocks and reduces hunger without adding calories. Also, meals require adequate volume to be satisfying, and fruits and vegetables provide more volume than other foods but with fewer calories. Take it from a doctor who's been treating overweight patients for twenty-five years. People don't get fat eating carrots.

But here's what's even more deceptive about glycemic indexes: they give the impression that starchy foods like bread and spaghetti are only a little worse than fruits and vegetables. In fact, as you will see, they are *much* worse.

Getting It Right: Glycemic Loads

Food scientists have recently developed a way to correct glycemic indexes for serving size. It's called the *glycemic load* and represents the effects on blood glucose of amounts of food people actually eat, rather than what goes on in the research lab. I can't overemphasize the importance of using glycemic loads instead of glycemic indexes. It changes the whole approach to avoiding glucose shocks. To understand why, look at the glycemic *loads* of the same five foods we looked at previously. Notice that in this list, typical serving sizes are specified:

Food (Serving Size)	Glycemic Load
Carrot (one 8-inch)	11
Tomato (one medium)	15
White bread (one ⅜-inch slice)	100
Spaghetti (1 cup)	166
Bagel (one medium)	340

Makes more sense, doesn't it? The rabbit food is at one end of the scale, the starchy stuff at the other. You can see why glycemic loads allow you to enjoy foods you might avoid if you let glycemic *indexes* be your guide.

But here's what's more important: *Correcting glycemic indexes for serving size exposes refined carbs as the culprits they really are.* Bagels, for example, aren't just a little worse than carrots, they're terrible! You would have to eat thirty raw carrots to get the glucose shock you get from one bagel.

Table 4.1 provides a list of the glycemic loads for typical servings of some common foods. (You'll find a more complete list in Appendix A.) How low should your daily glycemic load be? To stop your body from overproducing insulin, you need to keep your daily tally less than about 500. Generally, foods with ratings under 100 are OK; most people can eat satisfying amounts of these without gaining weight or raising their risk of diabetes. However, more than a couple of servings a day of foods with higher ratings drives up insulin levels, encourages weight gain, and raises the risk of diabetes.

Reducing Your Glycemic Load: A Simple Plan for Effective Weight Loss

All this glycemic-load business sounds very scientific, but if you look twice at the list of glycemic loads in Table 4.1, you can see what's going on. The culprits stand out in sharp relief. The foods with the highest glycemic loads (greater than 100) are ones most people would call "starchy": grain products, potatoes, rice, and soft drinks. You've just discovered the main sources of glucose shocks in the American diet, and now you know what you need to do. Get rid of those four foods, and the glycemic load of your diet will be a fraction of what it was. In fact, you don't even need a list of glycemic loads to tell you what to eat. Starch is never hidden. You can see it from across the room. The culprits are even color-coded for you: *they're the white foods.* The only other foods with glycemic loads as high as the starchy stuff are juices and soft drinks. So, if you cut out flour products, potatoes, rice, and sugar-containing beverages, you eliminate nearly all of the glucose shocks in your diet. Taking into account the minor glycemic loads you get from other foods, you can get away with eating the equivalent of about one full serving of starch a day. Here's my advice. Forget about lists. *Just don't eat more than a quarter serving of flour products, potatoes, or rice at a time, and abstain from sugar-containing soft drinks and fruit juices.* Oth-

Table 4.1 Glycemic Loads of Common Foods

Food Item	Description	Typical Serving	Glycemic Load
Pancake	5-in. diameter	2½ oz.	346
Bagel	1 medium	3⅓ oz.	340
Orange soda	8-oz. glass	12 oz.	314
White rice	1 cup	6½ oz.	283
White bread	2 slices, ⅜ in. thick	2¾ oz.	260
Baked potato	1 medium	5 oz.	246
Whole wheat bread	2 slices, ⅜ in. thick	2¾ oz.	234
Raisin bran	1 cup	2 oz.	227
Brown rice	1 cup	6½ oz.	222
French fries	Medium serving, McDonald's	5¼ oz.	219
Coca-Cola	12-oz. can	12 oz.	218
Hamburger bun	5-in. diameter	2½ oz.	213
English muffin	1 medium	2 oz.	208
Doughnut	1 medium	2 oz.	205
Cornflakes	1 cup	1 oz.	199
Macaroni	1 cup	5 oz.	181
Corn on the cob	1 ear	5⅓ oz.	171
Blueberry muffin	2½-in. diameter	2 oz.	169
Spaghetti	1 cup	5 oz.	166
Instant oatmeal (cooked)	1 cup	8 oz.	154
Chocolate cake	1 slice (4″ x 4″ x 1″)	3 oz.	154
Grape-Nuts	1 cup	1 oz.	142
Cheerios	1 cup	1 oz.	142
Special K	1 cup	1 oz.	133
Tortilla, corn	1 medium	1¾ oz.	120
Orange juice	8-oz. glass	8 oz.	119
Cookie (lab standard, 30 g)	1 medium	1 oz.	114
Grapefruit juice, unsweetened	8-oz. glass	8 oz.	100
White bread	1 thin slice, ¼-in. thick	1 1/16 oz.	100
Banana	1 medium	3¼ oz.	85
All-Bran	½ cup	1 oz.	85
Tortilla, wheat	1 medium	1¾ oz.	80
Apple	1 medium	5½ oz.	78
Orange	1 medium	6 oz.	71
Pinto beans	½ cup	3 oz.	57
Pear	1 medium	6 oz.	57
Pineapple	1 slice (¾″ x 3½″)	3 oz.	50
Peach	1 medium	4 oz.	47

Grapes	1 cup (40 grapes)	2½ oz.	47
Kidney beans	½ cup	3 oz.	40
Grapefruit	1 half	4½ oz.	32
Table sugar	1 round teaspoon	⅙ oz.	28
Milk (whole)	8-oz. glass	8 oz.	27
Peas	¼ cup	1½ oz.	16
Tomato	1 medium	5 oz.	15
Strawberries	1 cup	5½ oz.	13
Carrot (raw)	1 medium (7½-in. length)	3 oz.	11
Peanuts	¼ cup	1¼ oz.	7
Spinach	1 cup	2½ oz.	0
Pork	2 5-oz. chops	10 oz.	0
Margarine	Typical serving	¼ oz.	0
Lettuce	1 cup	2½ oz.	0
Fish	8-oz. fillet	8 oz.	0
Eggs	Typical serving	1½ oz.	0
Cucumber	1 cup	6 oz.	0
Chicken	1 breast	10 oz.	0
Cheese	1 slice (2" x 2" x 1")	2 oz.	0
Butter	1 tablespoon	¼ oz.	0
Broccoli	½ cup	1½ oz.	0
Beef	10-oz. steak	10 oz.	0

erwise, eat anything you want. There's not enough starch or sugar in the rest of your food to cause you much trouble. A weight loss program can't get any simpler than that. I will show you how to get rid of these "starchy fillers" and cushion the glucose shocks in starchy foods in the next chapter.

Opening the Door to a Richer, More Flavorful Way of Eating

Most low-carb diets go further than they need to in restricting fruits, vegetables, and sweets and even dairy products but not far enough in eliminating starch. Certainly, you can lose weight faster if you eliminate all carbs. However, weight loss comes at a high price in terms of satisfaction and healthiness. Such diets create irresistible food cravings. Most people just can't stay with them for long. To make up for restricting so many nutritious foods, many diets recommend taking vitamins, stool softeners, and various supplements. This is unnecessary if you only eliminate refined carbohydrates. No one in the history of the world has ever suffered any medical condition caused by lack of starch.

There's another bonus to reducing the glycemic load of your diet. Because starch is essentially tasteless, when you eliminate it you remove little in the way of flavor and texture, and you make room for other, tastier food. Starch no longer dilutes the taste of food. Instead of filling up on the same bland staples at every meal, you branch out to more flavor and richness. Eliminating starch will allow you to enjoy the pleasing qualities of a wider variety of foods. Don't be surprised if you find yourself eating *better* than you were before!

5

Job One: Purge Starch from Your Diet

Now you know why starch is public enemy number one. As soon as it hits your digestive tract, it turns to sugar and floods your bloodstream with glucose. These glucose shocks cause your pancreas to secrete excessive amounts of insulin, a notoriously obesity-promoting hormone. In this chapter, I'm going to pass on some tricks that will make eliminating glucose shocks and reducing your daily glycemic load easier for you.

Some of the advice I'm going to give you is based on my experience not only as a doctor but also as a patient. As a cardiologist, I followed the party line for years. I avoided cholesterol and ate plenty of refined carbohydrates. In 1999, I found out I had diabetes. As a doctor, I was well acquainted with the complications of poorly controlled diabetes such as eye, kidney, and blood vessel damage. Discovering I had this problem was akin to someone holding a gun to my head and telling me to keep my blood sugar down.

How I Became a Human Glycemic-Load Meter

The first thing I did when I discovered I had diabetes was buy a monitoring device so I could measure my blood glucose levels at home. In the past six years, I have checked my blood sugar thousands of times, after every kind of meal, snack, and physical activity. I can personally attest to the importance of the glycemic-load ratings. My blood glucose levels precisely reflect the glycemic loads of the foods I eat. As long as I avoid foods with high glycemic loads, my blood levels are fine. I don't have to think of much else. I can eat a full-course dinner of meat, vegetables, and salad, and my blood sugar hardly rises at all. I can even have some candy for dessert, and it still doesn't go up. However, if I eat so much as a single slice of bread or some potatoes, it skyrockets.

My low-glycemic-load eating style has been effective for preventing glucose surges and for losing weight. By my blood tests, no one could tell I am a diabetic, and I got rid of twenty pounds I needed to lose. The amazing thing is, I don't feel like I'm dieting or depriving myself at all. I avoid bread, potatoes, rice, and soft drinks but, for the most part, eat what I want.

Although I've never displayed much discipline when it comes to eating, I have not found lowering my glycemic load difficult to do. Truthfully, I eat better now than I did before. I assure you, a low-glycemic-load diet is a way of eating you can continue for life, even if you are not endowed with unusual willpower. I do it, my patients do it, and you can do it, too.

Strategies for Eliminating "Starchy Fillers"

The secret to eliminating glucose shocks is to "pick the low-lying fruit": concentrate on what reaps the most benefit with the least effort. Without question, the biggest bang for your buck—in fact, almost *all* the bang—comes from reducing your intake of what I call starchy fillers: bread, potatoes, and rice side dishes. These are by far the major offenders in most people's diets.

As deeply ingrained as the starch-with-every-meal habit is, starchy fillers are where we get most of our glucose shocks. The good news is that these are the easiest foods to eliminate. They're usually served as side dishes, not intended to be the highlight of meals. You don't miss out on any delicious entrées or draw attention to yourself by passing up the bread plate or leaving some potatoes on your plate. Because starch is mainly tasteless, when you remove it, you remove little in the way of flavor from your diet.

You also remove nothing in the way of essential vitamins, minerals, or fiber. This fact is important to remember, because diets deficient in vital nutrients inevitably trigger cravings for what's missing. There is no such thing as a "starch deficiency." Humans existed for millions of years without it, and our prehistoric ancestors were taller, stronger, and less susceptible to many diseases before starchy carbohydrates came on the scene.

Keep in mind that this is *not* a calorie-restricted diet. It's a way to avoid a substance that is toxic to you if you have insulin resistance. You can eat virtually everything else—meat, dairy products, nuts, fresh fruit, vegetables, even a little candy—and eat until you're satisfied. In fact, you don't even have to swear off bread, potatoes, and rice entirely. Just limit yourself to no more than a quarter serving at a time, or the equivalent to approximately one average-size helping a day.

Strategy 1: Pass Up the Bread Plate

No food is more deeply ingrained in American and European dietary tradition than bread. "Breaking bread" is synonymous with dining itself. It's part of religious rituals. We expect it with virtually every meal. But the plain truth is, our devotion to bread is killing us. You might recall from Chapter 2 that the skyrocketing obesity and diabetes rates in America in the last thirty years correlate precisely with our rising consumption of wheat products. The average American gets five to ten times more glucose shocks from bread and baked goods than from any other single food. So don't fall for the old trick restaurants play of enticing you to fill up on bread before the main dish arrives. Your first bite of food at a meal should never be a refined carbohydrate. When your stomach is empty, starch goes directly into your bloodstream and causes a huge glucose shock. If you want something to eat before the main dish arrives, have some real food—soup, salad, or an appetizer.

If *occasionally* you can't resist having some bread, wait until you finish the rest of your meal. That will allow time for the other foods to reach the appetite centers in your brain, and the fat and fiber in your meal will slow the entry of glucose into your blood-stream. Then eat just a little, a half slice at the most. Roll it around in your mouth a while before you swallow it. The longer your saliva works on it, the more glucose it releases in your mouth instead of your stomach, the more it stimulates your taste buds, and the more it will satisfy whatever craving you have for it. Put some butter or margarine on it if you want; this isn't a low-fat diet.

The reality is, if you are serious about eliminating glucose shocks, you must eliminate *all* bread in *all* forms: rolls, bagels, muffins, scones, crackers, sandwich bread, hamburger buns, and crusts. This is central to reducing the glycemic load of your diet. The good news is, if your diet is typical of what most Americans eat, that's almost all you have to do. The rest is easy.

The Whole-Grain Myth. What about whole-wheat bread? Isn't that supposed to be good for you? Indeed, real whole-*grain* bread—bread that contains whole kernels of grain—has more vitamins, protein, and fiber than white bread. Unfortunately though, when it comes to causing glucose shocks, a slice of whole-grain bread is just as bad as—in fact, slightly worse than—a slice of white bread.

Indeed, whole-grain bread breaks down to glucose slower than white bread does, so its glycemic *index* is slightly lower. However, those little kernels are packed with starch. Slice for slice, whole-grain bread contains up to twice as much starch as white bread. You simply get more food in a slice of whole-grain bread. The glycemic *load* of whole-grain bread—which takes into account the amount of carbohydrate in a typical serving—is actu-ally higher than that of white bread.

If you ate the same amount of carbohydrates in whole-grain bread as you did in white bread, you would, in fact, modestly reduce the size of the resulting glucose shock. But because whole-grain bread simply contains more carbs per slice than white bread, that would mean eating fewer or smaller slices. If you just substitute whole-grain for white bread without reducing the size or the number of the slices, you end up getting a larger glucose shock and more calories to boot.

Here's another problem with whole-grain bread. The modest reductions in glycemic *index* (not *load*) that researchers have reported for whole-grain breads are, in fact, for breads much higher in kernel content than the ones you're likely to find in a grocery store. Kernels accounted for 80 percent of the weight of the breads tested but make up less than 20 percent of most commercially available whole-grain breads. Brown bread, rye bread, and so-called whole-*wheat* (as opposed to whole-*grain*) bread contain less than 5 percent kernels.

Why don't supermarkets sell breads with higher kernel contents? It's a matter of palatability. Our ancestors learned thousands of years ago that the husks of grains have to be removed and the starchy cores pulverized to make them edible. A television journalist recently asked an owner of a bread company why manufacturers don't market breads with higher kernel contents. The company owner replied that people don't want bread that tastes like cardboard.

What about studies showing that people who eat whole-grain bread are healthier than people who eat white bread? Whole-grain consumption is a sign of someone who tries to live healthily. It doesn't mean whole-grain bread does them any good.

The Fiber Factor. One reason whole-grain bread has a reputation for being healthful is that the husks of wheat kernels contain *insoluble fiber*, an indigestible carbohydrate that helps prevent constipation and other colon problems. Indeed, the diets of most Americans and Europeans are grossly deficient in this nutrient. However, there isn't enough insoluble fiber in most whole-grain breads to make much of a difference—certainly not enough to make up for the glucose shocks you get. The recommended daily requirement for insoluble fiber is about twenty grams. A slice of whole-grain bread contains about two grams. By comparison, a half cup of bran cereal provides fourteen grams. You're better off getting your fiber from fruits, vegetables, and bran cereal than from bread.

Strategy 2: Push Aside the Potatoes and Rice

Imagine a pile of sugar on your plate the size of a baked potato or a serving of rice. The effect on your blood-insulin levels is the same. If you want to eliminate glucose shocks, you have to reduce your consumption of potatoes and rice.

Perhaps you're thinking that rice must be OK because Asians eat a lot of it and they're not as fat as Americans and Europeans are. Indeed, Asians have been eating rice for thousands of years. However, until the twentieth century, they consumed only small amounts of it. Rice kernels are difficult to extract from their husks. People had to grind it between stones and pick out the kernels by hand. Only the rich could afford to eat much of it. Only after the advent of rice-polishing machines in the 1920s did most Asians begin eating large amounts of it, and now they, too, are overweight. Asia has the fastest-rising incidence of obesity and diabetes in the world.

The trick to reducing your potato and rice consumption is to use these foods to stimulate your taste buds but not to satisfy your appetite. Wait until you finish eating the other food on your plate then take a few bites. Keep each bite in your mouth a while to get the full effect. You will find you only need a little—probably less than a fourth of a typical serving. Keep in mind as you eat them that even though they are largely tasteless, you might as well be eating sugar.

Cushioning the Glucose Shocks from Starch in Main Dishes

Avoiding starchy side dishes like bread, potatoes, and rice is easy enough. They're extras; you're not obliged to eat them. But what about the starch in main dishes like hamburgers, pizza, and pasta? Does eliminating refined carbohydrates mean you can't share meals with friends or eat in your favorite restaurants? Do you have to consult a food guide to find out how much starch is in the dishes you eat?

Interestingly enough, starch is rarely concealed. It's always right out in plain sight. There's no problem spotting the starch in a hamburger or piece of pizza. It's in the bun and crust. Moreover, starch is rarely *blended* with other ingredients. You can usually separate it from the rest of the dish with a few strokes of a knife and fork.

The plain visibility and separateness of starch reflects its distinct physical properties and the way it behaves in food preparation. In contrast, fat is usually invisible and blended with other ingredients. You have to consult a fat-gram counter to tell how much is in a dish, and once it's added, it usually can't be removed. One of the reasons low-carb diets are more effective than low-fat diets is that the culprits are so obvious. It's much simpler to avoid starch than fat. Here are some tricks for reducing the glycemic load of main courses.

Build a Starch Pile

Because the starchy parts of dishes are usually easy to see and separate from other ingredients, you can often pick them out as you eat. A good technique for reducing the glycemic load of meals is to build a pile on the side of your plate with the starch you remove from your food. Granted, starch is part of the appeal of some dishes. However, you can usually enjoy starch-containing dishes while eating a fraction of the starch they are served with if you simply pick some of the starch out as you eat and put it on your starch pile. After you finish the rest of your meal, if you still want some starch, you can take it from the pile. However, by then the other food will have had time to reach the appetite centers in your brain, and you won't be so ravenous. You'll probably find that seeing all that starch in a pile dampens your enthusiasm for it. As you leave the table, you can congratulate yourself on the size of the pile you left behind.

Use Other Foods to Slow the Absorption of Starch

When you can't avoid starch, you can cushion the glucose shock it causes by paying attention to the foods you eat with it and the order in which you eat them. Having other food in your stomach before eating refined carbohydrates reduces the size of the resulting glucose surge. Fat slows the digestion of starch, and fiber in fruits and vegetables acts like a kind of sponge, soaking up glucose and slowing its entry into your bloodstream. That's why it's smart to eat a salad before a meal and to avoid eating starch or sugar on an empty stomach.

Get Rid of the Sandwich Bread

Putting meat or cheese between slices of bread is a good way to make expensive food go further, but sandwiches are a major source of glucose shocks. Although they're a popular lunch food, there are plenty of alternatives. A salad with lots of rich ingredients—such as meat, cheese, nuts—will fill you up without causing a glucose shock. Most soups are fine if you leave some of the potatoes and noodles in the bowl. Soups and salads aren't as easy to pack for work as sandwiches are, but you can do it with plastic containers and a thermos bottle.

If you absolutely can't break the sandwich habit, try switching to wraps—sandwiches made with tortillas. A wheat tortilla has a glycemic load of 80, compared with 260 for two slices of white bread. Once you get the ingredients wrapped, you can usually tear away and discard about a fifth of the tortilla, which brings the rating down to about 70. If you use low-carb tortillas, the glycemic load is negligible.

Another major source of glucose shocks is hamburger buns (glycemic load of 213). Try skipping the bun altogether. You'll be surprised at how much better a piece of hamburger topped with all the extras is without the bread dough to dilute its taste. These days, restaurants are accustomed to serving burgers this way.

If you have to have some bun with your burger, you can reduce the glucose shock to more reasonable levels by removing half of it (preferably the top half because it's bigger). You can also make a good hamburger with a low-carb tortilla. The high fiber content of these tortillas soaks up fat from the meat, which moistens them and brings out a pleasing flavor. Cut a hamburger patty in half, fold the tortilla around it, and include all the extras. Low-carb tortillas also make good substitutes for hot dog buns.

Eat Your Pasta al Dente with Plenty of Amendments

Make no mistake, pasta is full of starch, and if you're trying to get rid of glucose shocks, you need to eat it sparingly. Fortunately, most of us don't eat pasta with every meal, as we do with bread, potatoes, and rice. Pasta also has some redeeming qualities that lessen its impact on your blood glucose. The starch in pasta turns to glucose in your intestinal tract more slowly than does the starch in other flour products such as bread. Pasta's effects on your blood glucose also depend on how you prepare it. The more you cook it, the faster it breaks down to glucose in your digestive tract, and the more it raises your blood glucose level. You can reduce the size of the glucose shock by eating pasta al dente—cooked less so it has a firmer texture. For example, the glycemic load of a cup of spaghetti boiled ten to fifteen minutes is 166. If you boil it for twenty minutes, the rating goes up to 213.

Another redeeming quality of pasta is that you can mix it with other ingredients, such as vegetables, meat, and olive oil. The more of the other ingredients you eat, the less pasta you consume, and the fat in meat and the fiber in vegetables slow the digestion of starch.

Whole-grain pastas generally have lower glycemic loads than regular pastas. For example, a cup of whole-grain spaghetti has a glycemic load of 126, compared with 166 for an equal-size serving of regular spaghetti. However, for most pasta lovers, the modest benefit of switching to whole grain doesn't make up for the sacrifice of taste and texture.

Removing Starch from Dishes After They're Served

If you remove the outer two inches of crust from a slice of pizza, you avoid about three-fourths of the breading. Just stick your knife under the topping, cut away a couple inches of crust, and put it on your starch pile. That will leave enough crust to provide a small piece to go along with each bite of topping. The glycemic load of the remaining quarter-slice of crust is about 20, not enough to cause a glucose shock, even if you have two or three slices.

Most casseroles are easy to handle. You can pluck out the potatoes or crust and put them on your starch pile. Rice casseroles are tougher. The best way to handle them is to serve yourself less rice and more of the amendments and push some of the rice to the side of your plate as you eat. Sometimes you have to be content with just lowering the amount of starch you get in entrées and not eliminating it. If your diet is typical, getting rid of the starchy *fillers*—the bread, potato, and rice side dishes—will get rid of most of the glucose shocks. If you just reduce the starch in main dishes by, say, half, the glycemic load of your diet will be a fraction of what it was.

Forget What You Saw on Television About Breakfast Cereals

Imagine you could make a food from the cheapest ingredients on earth and obtain a patent that gave you exclusive rights to sell it. Without competition, you could make a large profit—that is, if you could convince people to buy it. The best way to do that? *Advertise.*

You have been brainwashed. From the time you were old enough to sit in front of a television set, you were inundated by ads touting the deliciousness, health benefits, and fun to be had from eating breakfast cereals. Manufacturers put toys in cereal boxes to entice you. It only took a decade for television to change what we Americans ate for breakfast. We went from eating bacon and eggs to Wheaties and Cheerios. A generation of Americans grew up thinking cereals are "The Breakfast of Champions."

If you're trying to avoid glucose shocks, breakfast cereals are a *terrible* way to start the day. They are all made from grain, the most concentrated source of starch known, and a lot of them are laced with sugar to boot. Most cereals have unacceptable glycemic loads, including ones touted on television for their health benefits such as granola, Cheerios, raisin bran, and oatmeal. In one study, subjects fed instant oatmeal for breakfast consumed 80 percent more calories later in the day than did subjects fed omelets. Table 5.1 includes the glycemic loads of several popular breakfast cereals. In addition to containing sugar, many of these are sweetened with fructose, so glycemic-load measurements actually *underestimate* their impact. Remember, anything over 100 will give you glucose shock.

The Benefits of Wheat Bran. Fiber is the part of fruits and vegetables that your digestive system doesn't break down and absorb. It travels through your digestive tract and out in your stool intact. There are two kinds, soluble and insoluble. Each has its own health benefits. Soluble fiber acts like a sponge and soaks up sugar and fat, delaying their entry into your bloodstream. This kind of fiber reduces the glycemic load of other foods eaten with it, and is believed to help prevent obesity, diabetes, and gallbladder disease. Fruits and vegetables contain lots of soluble fiber.

Insoluble fiber works differently. It passes through your digestive tract as solid particles. This kind of fiber is valuable because

Table 5.1 Glycemic Loads of Popular Breakfast Cereals

Cereal	Serving Size	Glycemic Load
All-Bran	½ cup	85
Muesli	1 cup	95
Special K	1 cup	133
Cheerios	1 cup	142
Shredded wheat	1 cup	142
Grape-Nuts	1 cup	142
Puffed wheat	1 cup	151
Instant oatmeal	1 cup	154
Cream of Wheat	1 cup	154
Total	1 cup	161
Cornflakes	1 cup	199
Rice Krispies	1 cup	208
Rice Chex	1 cup	218
Raisin Bran	1 cup	227

it helps maintain normal bowel function. It's especially useful in relieving the *irritable bowel syndrome*, a condition most of us suffer from at times, characterized by alternating constipation and diarrhea, pellet-like stools, and uncomfortable gas. Insoluble fiber also helps prevent more serious bowel problems, including diverticulitis and colon cancer. Because insoluble fiber provides bulk for the digestive tract to work on, many experts think that lack of it promotes overeating.

In the Western diet, insoluble fiber is harder to come by than the soluble kind. Prehistoric humans consumed large amounts of it in grasses, roots, and unripe vegetation, but little remains in the modern diet. Consequently, diseases related to insoluble fiber deficiency have become increasingly common.

Although fruits and vegetables contain some insoluble fiber—mainly in their skins—we often don't eat enough for good bowel health. By far the most concentrated source of insoluble fiber in the Western diet happens to be the husk of the wheat kernel, the *bran*. But don't rush to the grocery store to buy whole-grain bread. Modern milling techniques remove almost all of the bran from wheat products, so most of the flour-based foods we eat are practically devoid of insoluble fiber. Even whole-grain bread falls short of providing adequate amounts.

One of the best ways to make sure you're getting enough insoluble fiber is to eat a high-fiber breakfast cereal. However, few breakfast cereals come close to providing enough insoluble fiber to justify the glucose shocks they cause. The only exceptions are 100 percent bran cereals, such as All-Bran. The glycemic load of a half cup of one of these cereals is 85, not quite enough to cause a glucose shock but enough to help make sure you're getting adequate insoluble fiber.

Table 5.2 includes the insoluble fiber contents for several popular breakfast cereals. Notice that many cereals touted as being high in fiber don't come close to providing as much fiber as All-Bran cereal does.

Be careful not to equate oat bran with wheat bran. Oat bran is a good source of *soluble* fiber but provides little *insoluble* fiber. It can actually worsen the symptoms of irritable colon syndrome.

Table 5.2 Insoluble Fiber Content of Breakfast Cereals

Cereal	Serving Size	Insoluble Fiber (grams)
All-Bran	½ cup	14
Fiber One	½ cup	13
Bran Buds	⅓ cup	10
Bran flakes	1 cup	6
Oat bran	⅓ cup	4
Raisin bran	½ cup	3
Cheerios	1 cup	2
Grape-Nuts	1 cup	2
Oatmeal	1 cup	2
Total	1 cup	2
Wheaties	1 cup	2
Rice Krispies	1 cup	1
Cornflakes	1 cup	1

Admittedly, 100 percent bran cereal is not most people's idea of exciting food. To liven up its taste, you can add some fruit, unsweetened yogurt, or a couple tablespoons of another breakfast cereal. Keep in mind that you don't have to have it for breakfast—you can eat it as a snack anytime.

What about bran muffins? Unfortunately, most commercially available bran muffins contain enough refined flour and sugar to cause a sizable glucose shock, and they don't provide nearly as much insoluble fiber as a serving of bran cereal. However, you can make your own high-fiber muffins by using less flour and more bran. You will find a recipe for low-glycemic-load, high-fiber muffins in the recipe section (in Chapter 13). One of those muffins will provide almost as much fiber as a bowl of bran cereal.

Don't Start Your Day with a Glucose Shock

When you eat starchy cereals or baked goods for breakfast, your blood glucose skyrockets and then crashes about four hours later, often causing symptoms of hypoglycemia such as tiredness, poor concentration, and exaggerated hunger. Starting the day with a glucose shock also makes you want to eat more later in the day. Researchers demonstrated this by feeding experimental subjects starchy breakfasts and comparing their food intake with that of a group fed an equal number of calories in low-starch breakfasts. Over the course of a week, those who ate the starchier breakfasts consumed 145 more calories at lunch and dinner than those who ate the less starchy ones. That's enough to make you gain sixty pounds in five years! It really is true: you're better off eating bacon and eggs.

6

Eliminate Sugar-Sweetened Beverages

Sugar in liquids behaves much differently in your body than sugar in solids. In solids such as candy, sugar interacts with your taste buds as you chew, which has an appetite-suppressing effect. In liquids, most of the sugar flows past your taste buds without stimulating them, which has much less of an appetite-suppressing effect. In one study, researchers fed sugar in the form of jelly beans to one group of subjects and sugar in a beverage to another group and then measured the subjects' food consumption afterward. The subjects who ate sugar in jelly beans curtailed their intake of other foods, but those who received sugar in beverages did not. In other words, *sugar in liquids adds calories rather than replacing calories from other foods.*

After sugar in solid food gets to your stomach, it has to wait its turn to be digested. In the meantime, it mixes with other foods, which slows its absorption. However, sugar dissolved in liquids bypasses the other foods in your stomach and releases glucose directly into your bloodstream. A sugar-sweetened beverage can cause a glucose shock in the middle of an otherwise low-glycemic-load meal. Even though sugar in liquids has less of an appetite-suppressing effect than sugar in solids, it actually raises blood glucose levels more.

A Glucose Shock in a Glass

In the list of glycemic loads in Chapter 4, you probably noticed that the only items with ratings as high as bread, potatoes, and rice are sugar-sweetened beverages and fruit juices. One glass of soda or fruit juice can raise blood glucose levels as high as a serving of starchy food. A twelve-ounce can of Coca-Cola has a glycemic load of 218. An eight-ounce glass of orange juice has a glycemic load of 119, and other fruit juices have even higher ratings.

Soft Drinks: A Major Source of Glucose Shocks

Pure sugar is overwhelmingly sweet. We tend not to eat much of it unless its sweetness is diluted or disguised—but dilute and disguise is exactly what soft drinks do. They dilute sugar with water and disguise its sweetness with sour ingredients, usually citric acid. Although most adults don't drink as much soda (the *non-diet* kind) as kids do, statistics show that those who consume even one glass a day double their risk of obesity and diabetes. In one study, women who drank one soda daily gained an average of twenty pounds in nine years.

These days, many soft drinks are sweetened with corn syrup, which contains high concentrations of *fructose*, a sugar that acts like glucose in your body. Americans are consuming much more fructose than they did thirty years ago, and some nutritionists suspect that this is playing a role in the obesity epidemic. You might read somewhere that fructose doesn't stimulate insulin, and that's true. It skips that step in your metabolism. Otherwise, it goes through the same metabolic pathways as glucose. Glycemic-index and -load measurements don't take fructose into account. If they did, the glycemic-load ratings of soda and fruit drinks would be even higher than they are.

If you want to lose weight, you must kick the soda habit. Fortunately, most grownups have little trouble giving up soda. There is one notable exception: people who have a cola addiction. I've encountered patients who drink ten or twelve cola drinks a day. Fortunately, these are often sugar-free colas, which suggests that something besides a craving for sugar drives the addiction, most likely an affinity for caffeine. The habit is harmless enough if the beverages are indeed sugar-free, but some cola freaks insist on sugar-sweetened ones, repeatedly assailing their bodies with glucose shocks. The best way to deal with this problem is to switch to sugar-free colas. Most cola slaves quickly adjust to the diet versions of their favorite beverages.

When it comes to glucose shocks, sugar-sweetened fruit drinks, including Snapple, SoBe, cranberry juice cocktail, Hawaiian Punch, and lemonade, and sports drinks like Gatorade are as bad as, or even worse than, sodas.

Most sugar-free diet drinks are carb-free and don't raise blood glucose or insulin levels. However, keep in mind that despite a fivefold per capita increase in diet-drink consumption in the last thirty years, the obesity rate has skyrocketed. Some nutritionists believe that artificial sweeteners desensitize people's taste buds to sweetness and cause them to overeat sugar in other foods.

Facing the Facts About Fruit Juice

Fruits in their natural forms are good for you. People who eat lots of fruit have fewer weight problems and less diabetes than people who don't. However, fruit *juices*, including orange and grapefruit juice, are another story, *even if they contain no added sugar*. Although fruit juice doesn't raise blood sugar quite as much as soda or sweetened fruit drinks do, research has linked regular consumption of fruit juice to obesity and diabetes.

Why would fruit in its natural form be good for you but fruit juice be harmful? Most of the sugar in a piece of fruit is in the juice. The squeezing process extracts the sugar from several pieces of fruit and puts it all in one serving of juice. In a sense, then, fruit juice *is* a sugar-sweetened beverage. The juice-making process also removes soluble fiber, which as I explained in Chapter 5, slows the absorption of sugar. Thus, the glycemic load of juice is always higher than that of the intact fruit. In addition, fruit juice, like soda, contains fructose, which glycemic-load measurements don't detect.

Although fruit juice raises blood glucose more than whole fruit does, it has less of an appetite-satisfying effect. Like other sugar-sweetened beverages, it adds to the calories provided by other foods, rather than replacing them. Orange juice, in particular, is a problem. We've been told since we were kids that it's good for us, but the truth is, it's a major source of glucose shocks and raises the risk of diabetes and obesity. My advice is to drink fruit juice only to satisfy a craving for something tangy, never to quench your thirst. If you have to have some juice, don't drink more than four ounces—a small glass—at a time.

Alcohol: Beware of Its Appetite-Stimulating Effects

Although beer, wine, and liquor are full of calories, the good news is that they actually don't raise blood glucose levels much. The fermenting process converts most of the sugar in these beverages to alcohol, which provides calories but requires no insulin to metabolize. However, alcohol blunts sensors in your brain that tell you when you have had enough to eat. A couple of drinks before a meal will make you tend to overeat. Alcohol can cause you to take in too many calories for another reason: it's addicting. If you're drinking more than one or two alcoholic beverages a day, you're getting enough calories from the drinks themselves to add pounds regardless of their glycemic effects.

Milk: Acceptable for Glycemic-Load Watchers

Americans are consuming less milk than they did thirty years ago, but the incidence of obesity and diabetes is skyrocketing. Recent studies show that people who consume generous amounts of dairy products have a *reduced* incidence of obesity and diabetes. The glycemic load of an eight-ounce glass of milk is only 27, making it a great drink for glycemic-load watchers.

Coffee and Tea: Good Beverages in Moderation

Coffee and tea are the most commonly consumed beverages in the world besides water. Scientists have studied them extensively and have never linked them to obesity. In fact, caffeine's stimulant effects encourage weight loss. Recent studies show a *reduced* incidence of type 2 diabetes among coffee drinkers.

Of course, too much coffee or tea can make you jittery and out of sorts as well as cause insomnia. Also, coffee stimulates stomach acid, which can increase hunger pangs and make you want to eat. Be sure you're not drinking so much as to cause these symptoms.

If you only drink a cup or two of coffee or tea a day, you don't have to worry about adding a little sugar. A teaspoon of table sugar has a glycemic load of 28—not enough to worry about. Artificial sweeteners are fine.

Water Is Great, but Do We Really Need Eight Glasses a Day?

Only recently in the span of human existence have people had containers to transport water or cups to drink it from. Prehistoric humans had to get down on their hands and knees to sip water from pools and streams. They didn't have beverages with every meal. They went for days without any liquids at all.

Nobody knows where the recommendation to drink eight glasses of water a day came from. There are no studies in the medical literature showing any benefit at all from drinking more water than you are naturally inclined to. Indeed, there's plenty of water in fruit, vegetables, meat, and dairy products, not to mention other beverages. Many people do just fine on a glass or two of liquid a day.

The idea that you should drink more water than you are naturally inclined to probably stems from the notion that it washes toxins out of the body, like running water over a bowl of lettuce to wash away the dirt. In fact, water in excess of what you need to survive doesn't even go into the cells of your body. You would die of water toxicity if it did. It goes directly to your kidneys and out in your urine.

Your body has powerful mechanisms for regulating water balance. The slightest decrease of your body's water content triggers compelling thirst and an outpouring of the hormone *vasopressin*, which provokes thirst and sharply reduces the amount of water that goes out in your urine. Unless you have a rare vasopressin deficiency, there's no need to consciously try to regulate your fluid intake. Your natural thirst mechanisms do the job just fine.

The simpleminded notion that filling your stomach with water makes you eat less is completely off base. Stretching the stomach with liquids just makes it empty faster and speeds the absorption of glucose. In fact, several things about the way liquids affect digestion suggest that excess water may actually *promote* weight gain. Laboratory animals deprived of water sharply curtail their food intake. Beverages consumed with a meal liquefy stomach contents and quicken their entry into the bloodstream. The more liquefied food is, the higher it raises blood glucose levels and the less it suppresses appetite.

My advice is that you make water your thirst quencher of choice (humans are the only animals on earth that drink anything *but* water), and let your thirst decide how much you drink.

7

Make Friends with Your Sweet Tooth

Many people think sugar is some kind of a poison, as if a teaspoon or two could expand into pounds of unsightly fat. The truth is, sugar is just another refined carbohydrate. A gram of it won't raise your blood glucose level any higher than a gram of carbohydrate in bread, potatoes, or rice. Although people seem to feel guilty about eating a few pieces of candy, they think nothing of consuming much more glucose in the form of starch. According to a recent dietary survey, the average American gets *twenty times* more glucose in grain products than in candy. Sweets are not what's making so many of us overweight these days. Americans don't eat any more candy per capita now than they did before the obesity epidemic began. The problem is starch.

Exonerating Sugar

The concept of glycemic load provides another valuable service to humanity: it exonerates sugar. To see how, compare the glycemic indexes of table sugar and peppermint candy with those of white bread and rice. Remember, these are glycemic *indexes*, not loads, so serving size is not specified:

Food	Glycemic Index
White rice	91
Table sugar	97
Peppermint candy	100
White bread	100

This table shows that fifty grams of carbohydrate in white bread or rice will raise your blood sugar as much as fifty grams of carbohydrate in sugar or peppermint candy, but in no way does it exonerate sweets. Sugar and candy appear to be just as bad as the starchy items. Now, in the following table look at the glycemic *loads*, which adjust for the amounts people typically eat:

Food (Serving Size)	Glycemic Load
Peppermint candy (1 Life Saver)	20
Table sugar (1 rounded teaspoon)	28
White bread (1 slice)	100
White rice (1 cup)	283

Paints a different picture, doesn't it? Sugar and peppermint candy have much lower glycemic loads than white bread and rice *simply because the typical serving sizes are smaller*. Most people don't eat nearly as much table sugar and peppermint candy in a typical serving as they do white bread or rice. This is true of other candies as long as the sugar in them is not diluted with starch. Consider chocolate. Ounce for ounce, chocolate releases about as much glucose in your bloodstream as a potato does. But how much chocolate can you eat? An amount the size of a potato? If you did, you would get a potato-size glucose shock. If you're trying to eliminate glucose shocks, a teaspoon of sugar in your coffee, a piece of peppermint candy, or a couple of squares of chocolate won't contribute much to your glycemic load. The reason people don't eat large amounts of sugar is that it's overwhelmingly sweet; you don't need much to satisfy your urge for it.

Unburdening Yourself of Sugar Phobia

It's ironic that we distrust sugar but regard starch as a natural food. Fruit is full of sugar. Anthropologists have found evidence that honey, which is 100 percent sugar, was more plentiful in prehistoric times than it is now. Early humans ate it for millions of years before starch came on the scene. Our tongues have taste buds that respond to sugar but none that interact with starch.

Paranoia about sugar probably stems from childhood. Sugar was the first food our parents warned us about, but it wasn't because they were worried about our getting fat. It was because they didn't want us to get tooth decay. Indeed, sweets can be bad for children's teeth; however, the problem is not so much candy itself as the frequency with which kids eat it. Acids from the bacterial breakdown of sugar in our mouths erode tooth enamel. Saliva neutralizes those acids and restores enamel, but the process takes several hours. When kids snack on candy and soda between meals, their saliva doesn't have time to counteract the acids, which eventually promotes tooth decay.

Part of people's misconceptions about sugar is a matter of semantics. Doctors have gotten in the habit of calling blood glucose "blood sugar," which leads people to think that the "sugar" in their blood comes from the sugar in sweets. In fact, the sugar in sweets is actually *sucrose*, a double molecule of glucose and fructose. The sugar in our blood is glucose, which for many of us comes mainly from starch.

How Sugar Can Help You Lose Weight

Sugar phobia plays into people's fears of obesity and diabetes, but the truth is, a spoonful or two of table sugar or a couple of pieces of candy a day contribute little to glycemic load, as you saw in the example of peppermint candy and white bread. In fact, when it comes to losing weight, sugar can be your ally. Here's how.

Starch Addiction

Although starch is a latecomer to the human diet and we have no biologically natural urge for it, many folks do seem to crave it. In my experience, most overweight people have more difficulty controlling their starch intake than they do their consumption of sweets or fat. That's why a book called *The Carbohydrate Addict's Diet* was a bestseller. What is it about starch that makes people crave it?

When the appetite-regulating centers in your brain want food, they want it fast, and nothing delivers calories into your bloodstream faster than starch. Consequently, we learn to associate starch with immediate satisfaction. We also learn to associate it with taste bud-stimulation. "Wait a minute," you're thinking, "didn't you just say that starch is tasteless?" Indeed, it is flavorless. However, saliva contains an enzyme called *amylase* that breaks down a small fraction of the starch in your mouth to glucose, which stimulates sweetness receptors on your tongue. The craving for starch, then, is a two-component urge: an impulse to quell hunger fast and a desire for stimulation of taste buds that sense sweetness.

Going for Real Taste-Bud Stimulation

You can satisfy your urge for starch without actually eating it by addressing the two components of your starch craving separately. The need for quick calories will dissipate if you just give other foods in your meal enough time to satisfy your hunger. If you postpone eating bread, potatoes, or rice until you have finished the rest of your meal, your desire for starch will lessen.

It may not go away, however. Although starch is a lousy taste-bud stimulant, chances are the other foods in your meal did not satisfy your sweetness receptors as much as some bread, potatoes, or rice could. Here's the best way to handle the desire for the taste-bud stimulation that starch provides: skip the bread and potatoes and go for the real thing, *sugar*. Wait until the end of your meal, and then, instead of the starch, have something sweet. That's right—eat dessert. A pinch of sugar will stimulate your taste buds more than a whole mouthful of starch. You'll find that your urge for starch quickly disappears. You'll finish your meal with your hunger *and* your desire for taste-bud stimulation satisfied.

Keeping Sugar in Its Place

We come by our urge for sweetness naturally. Our prehistoric ancestors ate it in pure form in honey for thousands of years before starch came on the scene. However, you can be sure they didn't eat too much of it. The surly nature of bees saw to that. Make no mistake, sugar is full of calories, and too much of it can cause your body to overproduce insulin, as any other refined carbohydrate can. It's just that sugar does a better job than starch does of stimulating your taste buds, curbing your appetite for other foods, and offsetting the calories it adds. Here are some suggestions for making friends with sugar:

- **Avoid "starchy" sweets.** The good news if you have a sweet tooth is that you can enjoy sweets in moderation, as long as they aren't *starchy* ones. For example, a one-inch square of quarter-inch-thick dark chocolate has a glycemic load of 39, which is minor. A couple of pieces won't cause a glucose shock. The sugar in chocolate isn't diluted with tasteless starch, so you get to savor every bit of it, which can be tremendously satisfying if you crave something sweet. Other low-starch sweets include jelly beans, peanut brittle, peanut M&M's, and hard candy.

  Cookies, cakes, and pies are another matter. They're full of starch, which passes into your stomach without rousing your taste buds, requiring you to eat more of it to satisfy your sweet tooth. A typical serving of a baked good releases several times more glucose into your bloodstream than a piece of chocolate does.
- **Use sweets only to stimulate your taste buds, not to satisfy hunger.** The key to making peace with your sweet tooth is to use sweets only to stimulate your taste buds,

not to satisfy your hunger. Can you eat too much of these things? You bet you can. And it's a fact that some sweets taste so good, you tend to overeat them even when you're not hungry. Try to keep in mind that sugar is like nuclear power: it can be a powerful tool, but you have to use it properly. A good rule is to eat only as much as you can wrap your fingers around.

- **Go sugar-free when eating dairy treats.** Sugar-containing dairy products like ice cream, sweetened yogurt, and cheesecake pose a unique problem. Although they contain no starch, they dilute and disguise sugar in the same way soft drinks do. Sugar-sweetened yogurt, cheesecake, and ice cream can give you a glucose shock; whereas no-sugar-added yogurt, cheesecake, and ice cream will not. (Don't make the mistake of confusing *sugar-free* with *low-fat* ice cream or yogurt. These products may have less fat but usually have unacceptable glycemic loads.)

- **Substitute rich, sugarless snacks.** If you want something to munch on and you don't care for sweetness, there are plenty of satisfying sugarless snacks. One of the healthiest is nuts. They are full of protein, fiber, and essential fatty acids, and their glycemic loads are negligible.

The reality is if you love sweets, it's foolish to try to live without them. Indeed, sugar can add pleasure to your life without necessarily causing harm. Just avoid starchy sweets, use candy to stimulate your taste buds and not to satisfy hunger, and don't eat more than a fistful.

8

Activate Your
Slow-Twitch Muscles

Maria, age twenty-eight, couldn't understand why she had gained seventy pounds in the last three years. She didn't think her diet had changed. She worked at a computer all day but had been doing that for several years. The only change in her life was that she moved to the suburbs and started driving to work instead of walking. Before that, she walked a mile to and from work every day. Maria had a hard time believing that walking to work instead of driving was what had kept her from gaining weight.

Bob had gained fifty pounds in ten years during which he worked as a computer programmer. At age forty-two, he developed type 2 diabetes. When he reduced his starch and sugar intake and started exercising on weekends, he lost twenty pounds, and his blood glucose measurements improved. However, he found it difficult to lose more weight. Then he had an idea. He started having his wife drop him off two miles away from his office so he could walk to work every day. He lost twenty more pounds in a year.

I have often been astonished by the weight loss benefits of walking to work every day. What is it about regular, low-intensity exercise that relieves insulin resistance so effectively?

You Can Gain Without the Pain

It's not your liver, kidneys, or some other internal organ that causes insulin resistance. It's your *muscles*. Their lack of responsiveness to insulin makes your pancreas secrete six to eight times the normal amounts of the hormone to handle the carbohydrates you eat. The good news is that you can restore your muscles' sensitivity to insulin. You do it with exercise, but not the kind you're probably thinking of, not the sweaty, exhausting kind. When it comes to reversing insulin resistance, the benefits of exercise don't necessarily correlate with strenuousness.

Let me illustrate this with a story. A group of researchers in Switzerland worked in a clinic near a mountain. There were two ways to get to the top—you could traverse a two-mile path or ride a tram. The scientists decided to compare the effects on blood sugar of walking up the mountain and riding the tram down versus taking the tram up and walking down. After two months, they measured their subjects' responses to a glucose load. To the researchers' surprise, walking downhill improved insulin sensitivity more than walking uphill did.

The point is, the no-pain, no-gain philosophy of exercise doesn't always apply. Certainly, if you're training for a footrace or trying to build big muscles, you need to sweat and strain, and walking uphill would be better than walking down. However, some kinds of muscle activity create less fatigue than others do, and if you're trying to relieve insulin resistance, it so happens this is exactly the kind you need. To understand how this is so, you need to consider what causes insulin resistance.

The Genetic Defect Underlying Insulin Resistance

Researchers have recently pinpointed the biochemical quirk that causes some people's muscles to lose sensitivity to insulin when they don't exercise enough. It's a genetic defect in the tiny energy-producing units of muscles called *mitochondria*. These little dynamos use oxygen to burn glucose and fat and produce the energy that powers muscles.

The difference between people who are genetically prone to developing insulin resistance and those who are not is that the mitochondria of those predisposed to insulin resistance go into a deeper than normal dormant state when they haven't been used. It's like my computer. If I don't use it for an hour, it automatically goes into "sleep mode." It's not completely shut off; parts of it are still running, and if I press a key, it immediately starts up again. But while it's in the sleep mode, it uses less energy.

That's the way your muscles behave if you have insulin resistance. If you don't use them for a day or two, they go into a kind of sleep mode in which they burn fewer calories and stop responding to insulin. When you exercise them again, they immediately wake up. They remain sensitive to insulin for twenty-four to forty-eight hours, and then they shut back down.

The message should be clear. If you keep your muscles from going into sleep mode—by exercising them every twenty-four to forty-eight hours—they will maintain their sensitivity to insulin, your pancreas won't have to make as much insulin, and your body will stop trying to store calories as fat.

Muscles That Don't Fatigue

To understand how it's possible to keep your metabolism humming like a long-distance runner's but without a lot of huffing or puffing, you need to know about the two different kinds of muscle fibers in your body. Your muscles comprise a mix of two different types of muscle fibers. One kind contracts slower than the other does, so they're called "slow-twitch" fibers. The others are "fast-twitch" fibers. Each type specializes in its own kind of exercise. Slow-twitch fibers provide power for steady, long-distance activities like walking or jogging. You use fast-twitch fibers for short bursts of intense effort like weight lifting or sprinting.

The important difference between these two kinds of muscle fibers is that slow-twitch fibers require oxygen to do their work, and fast-twitch fibers do not—at least not immediately. They go into "oxygen debt," replenishing their energy after their work is completed.

Because slow-twitch fibers need more oxygen while they're working than fast-twitch fibers do, they have more mitochondria, which, as you recall, *is exactly where the problem is if you have insulin resistance.* That's why exercise like walking or jogging, which depends on slow-twitch fibers, promotes weight loss better than short bursts of more strenuous exertion like weight lifting, which use mainly fast-twitch fibers.

You may find it hard to believe that you can lose weight without strenuous exertion, but think for a moment about your diaphragm, the muscle under your rib cage that moves air in and out of your lungs. How much effort does it take to exercise that muscle to breathe? You're not even aware you're doing it. Indeed, certain muscles can work steadily for long periods without causing fatigue. The reason such muscles can operate without producing a sense of tiredness is that they're powered by slow-twitch muscle fibers. As slow-twitch fibers work, oxygen constantly replenishes their energy.

A light should have just come on in your brain: *slow-twitch fibers are where the problem is if you have insulin resistance.* How convenient! The kind of exercise you need to restore your body's sensitivity to insulin is exactly the kind that requires the least effort. You don't need to sweat and strain to lose weight. All you have to do is turn on those oxygen-burning mitochondria in your slow-twitch muscle fibers. Here's how to do it.

Keeping Your Slow-Twitch Fibers Out of "Sleep Mode"

Because all animals need to breathe and get from one place to another, Mother Nature made sure that the muscles that perform those tasks operate with as little effort as possible. Consequently, those activities rely almost entirely on slow-twitch muscle fibers. Of course, your breathing muscles are only a small part of your total muscle mass, so they contribute little to your metabolism. But the muscles that propel you, your walking muscles, are a different story. They represent about 70 percent of your muscle mass. Activating them has a profound effect on your body chemistry. And that's where the problem lies: modern humans are the only creatures in the history of the world who don't depend on muscle power to get from one place to another.

Although a change in dietary habits triggered the rise in obesity of the last thirty years, the stage was set by the marked reduction in muscle activity that occurred over the previous century as engines took over the task of moving us from one place to another. Think about how little we modern folks walk compared with our ancestors. Prehistoric humans spent most of their waking hours scrambling across rugged terrain in search of food and game. They migrated hundreds of miles as the seasons changed. As recently as the early 1900s, people thought nothing of walking four or five miles a day to get to and from their jobs and spent most of their workday on their feet. Now it's a big deal if you have to walk across a parking lot or up a flight of stairs. We use our walking muscles a pitiful fraction of what our ancestors did.

Considering that most of the mitochondria in our bodies reside in our walking muscles, it's not surprising that our metabolisms are out of whack. The reason so many of us are insulin resistant is not that we don't go to health clubs, lift weights, or run marathons. It's because we don't walk. We don't use our slow-twitch muscle fibers enough to keep them out of sleep mode.

The Optimal Oxygen-Burning Pace

Our ancestors walked simply to get from point A to point B. They weren't doing it to keep in shape. They didn't have to push themselves. You don't have to push yourself either.

The next time you go for a walk, pay attention to how much effort you're expending. If you walk fast enough, you become air-hungry, and your legs start to feel tired. If you're not an exercise lover, you might describe that as strenuous. But notice what happens when you decrease your walking speed just a little. You will find that you don't have to slow down much before the shortness of breath and leg fatigue abruptly stop. You quickly reach a point where you don't sense you're expending much effort at all. What's happening? That's the level of exertion at which the energy you expend powering your slow-twitch muscle fibers is being completely replenished by oxygen. You aren't pushing your muscles beyond their capacity, and you're not building up an oxygen debt by enlisting your fast-twitch fibers. You stop thinking about how hard you're working, and your mind moves on to other things. At that pace, you feel as if you could walk indefinitely. You might be bored, you might be in a hurry to get home, but you cannot honestly say that what you're doing is strenuous. *That is all the effort you need to expend to relieve insulin resistance and lose weight.*

Make no mistake, there are benefits to more strenuous exercise—you can build more endurance and develop stronger muscles. But remember what you're trying to accomplish. You're not training for a footrace or trying to build big muscles. You're just trying to restore your muscles' sensitivity to insulin, and happily, there's a disconnect between strenuousness of exercise and its effectiveness for reversing insulin resistance. You don't have to push yourself. All you have to do is take yourself back to the nineteenth century and use your leg muscles as nature intended, to walk at a comfortable pace.

Turning on Your Metabolic "Switch"

If it's inconvenient to walk—if the weather's bad or if you can't find a place to do it—you can activate your slow-twitch muscle fibers with a StairMaster, elliptical trainer, or stationary bike. For easiness, however, there's nothing better than walking. Exercise physiologists have found that of all the different kinds of exercise, walking burns the most calories with the least *perceived* effort. In other words, you might not think you're exercising much, but you really are. Study after study proves that for losing weight and preventing diabetes, walking is just as effective as running or working out at a gym.

Exercise activates biochemical reactions in muscles that allow them to respond to insulin. As you would expect, you can't get these reactions going by sauntering over to the watercooler. You need to exercise for a certain amount of time. The question is how long you have to walk to relieve insulin resistance.

Insulin sensitivity exhibits a sort of all-or-none phenomenon —like a switch, it's either on or off. Once you do enough exercise to get those metabolic processes started, there's little need to do more. You've already learned that you don't have to engage in strenuous exercise to activate your slow-twitch fibers. Walking at a comfortable pace is just fine. Now, if you could figure out the minimum amount of walking needed to switch on your insulin sensitivity, you could get away with doing that and no more.

Researchers have found that it takes between twenty and thirty minutes of walking to switch on insulin sensitivity. Exercising more than that might be good for other things—you might burn more calories or get in better shape—but it's unnecessary if you're just trying to lose weight.

Research studies show that the weight loss benefit of going from being a couch potato to walking just twenty minutes every other day is greater than the benefit of going from walking regularly to being a long-distance runner. Nevertheless, as long as you're out there walking, you might want to do enough to guarantee that you shed pounds. Most studies show that people consistently lose weight—even if they don't change their diet—if they *walk forty minutes four times a week*. That's about two miles every other day.

The Forty-Eight-Hour Rule

Whatever you do to reverse insulin resistance, you need to do it at least every other day. It doesn't matter if you walk a couple of miles or run a marathon. About forty-eight hours later, your muscles stop responding to insulin. Exercising only on weekends, even if it's very vigorous, won't do the trick.

Considering that the beneficial effects of exercise last only forty-eight hours, if you have a sedentary job and exercise only on weekends, your body spends four days a week in a state of insulin resistance. That means for four days out of seven, you have higher than normal insulin levels, your weight-regulating systems are out of kilter, and your body tries to store calories as fat.

Relatively sedentary activities like walking around an office, retrieving files, or doing light housework are no substitute for aerobic exercise, but if such movements are performed hundreds of times a day, they contribute significantly to energy expenditure.

Conversely, the fewer such movements you make throughout the day, the greater your tendency to gain weight. Researchers call this the *fidget factor*, and it significantly influences your ability to lose weight.

Two common activities have very low fidget factors: working on a computer and watching television. Observe someone doing these things. They hardly move a muscle for several minutes at a time. Television screens and computer monitors seem to mesmerize people, freezing their body movements. Some of the worst physically conditioned people I see in my medical practice are computer workers. So if you spend more than eight hours a day in front of a computer or television screen, walking every other day might not be enough. You probably need to exercise daily.

Enhancing the Pleasure and Comfort of Walking

Chances are you'll enjoy walking for its own sake. It provides a respite from day-to-day hassles, gives you some time to gather your thoughts, and puts you in touch with the physical world. Regular walking stimulates the body's natural antidepressant hormones and is actually as effective as medication for relieving mild depression.

However, if walking isn't entertaining enough, modern technology can help. A portable CD or MP3 player will allow you to listen to music, lectures, or audio versions of books as you walk. One devoted hoofer told me she gets so engaged listening to audiobooks that she often extends her route so she can listen longer.

If you're starting a walking program for the first time, I suggest you buy a couple of heel pads at your local drugstore and wear them for a month or two as your feet toughen up. The most common cause of persistent foot pain upon starting a walking program is something called *plantar fasciitis*, which causes painful heels. The pads will help prevent that.

If walking makes the balls of your feet or your big toe joint hurt, try a pair of cheap arch supports, which you can buy at most drugstores. They redistribute the pressure on your feet and help prevent soreness.

The rewards of walking? If you add forty minutes of slow-twitch muscle activation every other day to a low-glycemic-load diet, your body will work much differently than it did before. Your insulin levels will drop like a rock, your triglyceride level will plummet, and your body's natural antidepressant hormones will surge. Immediately, you'll feel better, and soon you'll start looking better.

9

Avoid Diet-Induced Metabolic Shutdown

None of us wants to deprive ourselves of the enjoyment of food. We'll go on a diet to lose weight, but we want it to be over as quickly as possible. We approach weight loss with a fix-it mentality. We want to get the job done and return to business as usual as quickly as possible. Our usual strategy, then, is to put ourselves through a period of deprivation until we reach a goal and then to go back to our old ways, with minor modifications to maintain weight loss. At least that's the plan— and that's the problem.

Without a doubt, the greatest obstacle to successful weight loss is the concept of "dieting," the idea of putting yourself through a period of deprivation that ends when the goal is reached. As rational as that strategy might seem—and we persist in trying it over and over again—it virtually guarantees failure.

Crash Dieting: A Metabolic Train Wreck

Most doctors, nutritionists, and diet book authors know that rapid-weight-loss diets usually fail. People shed pounds initially but usually gain them back *plus more*. Why then, you might ask, do they persist in recommending this approach? Because it's what people *expect*.

Two popular low-carb diets, Atkins and South Beach, recommend kicking their regimens off with a period of strict carbohydrate restriction called "induction phases." Purportedly, the idea is to purge dieters' carb cravings—like putting an alcoholic in a detox ward to get him off booze. This near-total carbohydrate restriction causes substantial weight loss in just a week or two. Although much of that is water loss and not true fat depletion, its real purpose is to boost dieters' morale and give them an incentive to continue. It also inspires them to spread the word of how effective their latest diet is.

Call these regimens what you will, they're crash diets, the same old failed strategy of starving weight off with a strict diet that is not intended to be maintained. This approach to weight loss contains the seeds of its own destruction. Here's why.

Crash dieting of any kind—whether low-carb or low-fat—throws your body chemistry into a sort of starvation mode. Within a few days, your metabolism starts to fight back. Powerful hormonal reactions slow your metabolism to prevent weight loss. This slowdown deepens over the course of weeks, making it increasingly difficult to lose weight. But here's the really bad news: diet-induced metabolic slowdown doesn't go away when you stop dieting. It continues after you return to normal eating, making it almost inevitable that you gain back the weight you lost. The worst of it is, this starvation mode persists after you regain the weight you've lost, encouraging you to gain even more weight. Alas, most crash diets result in weight *gain*, not loss. The word *crash* is appropriate: it's a metabolic train wreck!

Crash diets and induction phases are wrong for another reason. They restrict nutritious foods. After a week or two, dieters start craving what they're missing. These cravings, combined with diet-induced metabolic slowdown, practically guarantee failure.

The Ketosis Myth

Atkins and others in his time were impressed with a phenomenon called *ketosis*. If you eliminate all carbohydrates, after several hours, your body starts converting fat and protein to glucose. This process produces natural chemical by-products called *ketones*. Some of these substances end up in your urine and can be detected with a simple chemical test.

Atkins advocated restricting carbs until ketones appeared in the urine. He thought this meant that people were literally flushing calories down the drain—an attractive notion, indeed, but one that has since been disproved. The amount of calories you lose this way is inconsequential. Researchers have put subjects on low-starch diets with enough carbohydrates in fruits and vegetables to prevent ketosis and have found little difference in weight loss from that produced by near-total carbohydrate restriction.

A Role for Resistance Exercise

As crucial as moderate, continuous exercise like walking or jogging is for improving insulin sensitivity and shedding pounds, resistance exercise such as weight lifting has a special role in preventing the metabolic slowdown that accompanies rapid weight loss. Strict diets cause muscles to shrink, which reduces the number of calories they burn during exercise *and* rest and contributes heavily to diet-induced metabolic slowdown.

Resistance exercise—brief, intense effort against resistance— is superior to other kinds of exercise for building and maintaining muscle mass. Scientists have determined that resistance exercise helps to counteract diet-induced metabolic slowdown. If you find that you are losing weight fast—say, more than seven pounds the first month or four pounds a month thereafter—it's a good idea to add some resistance exercises to your aerobic program.

How much weight lifting does it take to make a difference? The beauty of resistance exercise is that it only has to be done for a few minutes a week to build and maintain muscle mass, as long as *effort is expended against maximum resistance*. The following twice-a-week, fifteen-minute routine is possible to do quickly at the gym or at home and has been proven by exercise physiologists to do the job:

- **Three exercises for the arms:** biceps curls, triceps presses, and shoulder lifts.
- **Three exercises for the legs:** knee extensions, hamstring curls, and squats.
- **For each muscle group:** Do two sets of ten repetitions, the first set against 80 percent of the maximum weight you can lift ten times, and the second set against 100 percent of the maximum weight you can lift ten times.

Most gyms have equipment designed for this kind of exercise, but you can get a similar workout with a pair of extra-heavy dumbbells.

Remember that weight loss tends to slow your metabolism, while exercise revs it up—and not just while you're doing it, but twenty-four hours a day. Weight lifting works by preserving muscle mass. Aerobic exercise like walking or jogging works by increasing the size and number of mitochondria in your slow-twitch muscles and enhancing your body's sensitivity to insulin.

Debunking the Myth of Rapid Weight Loss

You've seen the ads suggesting you can diet away thirty or forty pounds in a few weeks. The truth is, that kind of weight loss is usually a combination of dehydration, muscle shrinkage, inaccurate measurement, and self-delusion. If you came anywhere near losing that much fat that fast, you would shut your metabolism down for years. Rapid weight loss invariably sets you up for equally rapid weight gain.

How much weight loss can you reasonably expect? Cutting out starch and sugar typically causes about three pounds of water loss and two pounds of fat loss the first month. Walking two miles every other day burns off another two pounds. That makes seven pounds the first month and four pounds a month thereafter. That's enough! If you lose more than that, you risk shutting down your metabolism.

Heading Off Metabolic Shutdown Before It Hits

Scientists can detect metabolic slowdown within a few days of starting a strict diet. Some slowing probably occurs within a few hours, which would suggest that it's important not to skip meals. While scientists have not yet discovered the internal signal that triggers diet-induced metabolic slowing, undoubtedly, a sense of hunger accompanies it. To keep your body chemistry humming, you need to keep the metabolic furnaces stoked. You should answer the call of hunger.

Scientists have recently discovered that low-glycemic-load diets cause less metabolic slowing than low-fat diets do. Making a point of including some fat in your diet helps avoid diet-induced metabolic slowdown.

Unless you visit a research laboratory every day, it's impossible to tell if your body chemistry is slowing down. The best strategy is to prevent diet-induced metabolic slowdown before it occurs. Here are some suggestions:

- Rid yourself of the "dieting" mentality. Make modest changes you can stick with permanently.
- Avoid rapid weight loss (more than seven pounds the first month or four pounds a month thereafter).
- Do not try to lose weight by reducing food intake alone. Always add aerobic exercise like walking or jogging.
- Maintain adequate fat intake.
- Don't skip meals.
- Add resistance exercise if you find yourself losing more than three or four pounds a month.

If you only lose a couple of pounds a month but you're comfortable doing it, you'll know you've found a healthier way of living you can continue for life. Confidence is the key. When you're sure you have the right strategy, you stick with it.

Part 3

Strategies to Balance
Your Metabolism and
Stay on Track

10

Crafting a Fat-Balancing Strategy

To lose weight, the only thing you need to know about fat is that too much of it can add pounds. However, the food we eat contains several kinds of fat, and each type has unique effects on our body chemistries. Scientists are not yet sure of the importance of these effects, but because humans lived for millions of years on diets with a particular balance among various kinds of fats, you should be aware of the differences. Also, a change in the balance of fats in your diet can influence your cholesterol level. Although these effects are usually modest, sometimes they *are* significant, so they're worth knowing about.

Remember, though, for you to lose weight, your top priority must be to eliminate refined carbohydrates. Avoid being sidetracked by fat and cholesterol hang-ups. The wider the variety of foods you have to choose from, the easier it will be to cut starch and sugar. However, if you can improve the balance among the fats in your diet without compromising your weight loss program, you just might be healthier for doing it.

The Differences Between "Bad" and "Good" Fats

The first distinction you should make is between *saturated* and *unsaturated* fat, so-called "bad" and "good" fat. You can actually tell the difference just by looking at them. Saturated fats are solid at room temperature; unsaturated fats are liquid.

Most of the saturated fat in our diet comes from the visible fat in meat (the *suet*) and the fat in milk products (the *butterfat*). The other kind of fat, unsaturated fat, comes from oily plant foods like nuts, soybeans, olives, and avocados, as well as eggs, dairy products, and meat. The reason it's important to distinguish between saturated and unsaturated fat is that excessive amounts of saturated fat can raise blood cholesterol, while unsaturated fat usually does not. In fact, certain kinds of unsaturated fat actually *lower* cholesterol.

If you reduce your intake of saturated fats and increase your consumption of unsaturated fats, your cholesterol level will usually decline modestly, on average between 5 and 10 percent. However, results are variable. Your level might fall more than that or not at all. Often cholesterol goes down initially and then goes back up after a few months.

Mono- Versus Polyunsaturated Fats

There are two kinds of unsaturated fats—*monounsaturated* and *polyunsaturated*. Both are oils, so you can't tell the difference by simply looking at them.

Monounsaturated fats are somewhat hard to come by. We get them mainly from certain oily plant foods—namely, olives, nuts, and avocados. Polyunsaturated fats are more abundant. Vegetable oils, including corn, soybean, and peanut oil, as well as meat and fish contain plenty of polyunsaturated fats.

Monounsaturated fats actually lower bad cholesterol slightly and raise good cholesterol. Many nutritionists believe that these fats are good for the heart and blood vessels. Inhabitants of some countries where olive oil provides a large portion of the fat they eat have a lower incidence of heart disease than do people from parts of the world where olive oil is not such a large part of the diet. However, other factors may explain those differences.

Polyunsaturated fats also lower bad cholesterol levels a little, but they lower good cholesterol too. Their net effect, although probably not harmful, is likely not beneficial either.

Getting Your Omega-3 Fatty Acids

When your body needs a particular type of fat, it can usually convert other kinds to whatever type it requires. However, your system can't manufacture certain kinds of important fats, so you have to rely on dietary intake to provide them. Because it's essential that you get these fats in your food, they're called *essential fatty acids*. Your body uses them to make cell membranes, hormones, and other important things.

The hardest kind of essential fatty acid to come by is a type of polyunsaturated fat called *omega-3 fatty acid*. Humans aren't alone in being unable to manufacture omega-3s. No member of the animal kingdom can. Only certain plants synthesize them, mainly leaves, grasses, and algae. Because we don't eat these kinds of plants, we get most of our essential fatty acids from the meat of animals that do, including grass-eating animals like cattle and sheep, and fish that consume smaller algae-eating creatures.

In the past, we got enough omega-3 in the meat we ate. However, these days, instead of allowing cows and sheep to graze on natural foliage, ranchers confine them to feedlots and fatten them up with grain, which contains little omega-3 fatty acid. As a result, our diets are becoming increasingly deficient in this nutrient. There is little doubt we modern humans are eating less than our ancestors did. Although there are no common diseases known to be caused by omega-3 deficiency, many experts believe that supplementing the diet with it has beneficial effects on the heart and blood vessels.

The best source of omega-3 fatty acids is certain cold-water fish, including salmon and sardines. Walnuts and flaxseed oil also are good sources. A couple of fish oil capsules, a handful of walnuts a day, or two servings of cold-water fish a week—what the American Heart Association recommends—should assure adequate intake.

The Trans Fat Controversy

Polyunsaturated fat becomes rancid after a few days of exposure to air at room temperature, which limits its commercial use. Food manufacturers learned to get around this problem by using a process called *partial hydrogenation*, heating the oil for several hours in the presence of hydrogen gas. Partial hydrogenation extends the shelf life of baked goods and margarines made with vegetable oil. If you look at the label on packages of cookies, crackers, chips, or margarine, you'll usually find the phrase "partially hydrogenated oil."

After food scientists discovered that polyunsaturated fat did not raise cholesterol, they began recommending that people consume more of it and less saturated fat. For years, folks thought they were doing themselves a favor by eating products made from polyunsaturated fats instead of butterfat and lard, and the food industry changed to accommodate this preference. Then, in the 1990s, scientists discovered a problem. The high temperatures used during partial hydrogenation damaged polyunsaturated fat, changing some of it to an unnatural kind of fat called *trans fat*. Trans fat raises blood cholesterol levels almost as much as butter and lard do.

Medical science isn't yet sure what kinds of problems trans fat can cause. The American Heart Association still recommends unsaturated over saturated fat but suggests limiting consumption of margarines and partially hydrogenated oils until scientists learn more about them. The good news is that if you concentrate on reducing your glycemic load, you don't have to worry about trans fat. That's because cutting out refined carbohydrates gets rid of the shortening, cooking oil, margarine, and butter you consume to make starch palatable. Most of the partially hydrogenated fat in our diet is in the starch we eat. When you cut out commercially prepared cookies, crackers, and chips, you get rid of the partially hydrogenated oils that go with them, and when you eliminate bread, potatoes, and rice, you no longer need margarine to make them taste better.

Improving the Quantity and Quality of Fats in Your Diet

Atkins proved to the world that people can eat fatty foods and still lose weight. You might ask, then, why you should pay attention to your fat intake. Here's the best reason. Not going overboard on fat makes room in your diet for fruits, vegetables, and sweets, and it's the lack of those foods that foils most people's attempts to stay on a low-carb diet.

The good news is, if you eliminate starch, you usually don't have to *consciously* avoid fat. That's because cutting out refined carbohydrates gets rid of the shortening, cooking oil, margarine, and butter you consume to make starch palatable. You experience a pleasant paradox: you can eat more meat, dairy products, nuts, and olives than you did before without actually increasing your fat consumption. It might seem like you're eating more fat, but you're not. Research studies have shown repeatedly that people on low-carb diets who eat all the eggs, meat, and dairy products they want end up consuming fewer calories on average than people on low-fat diets *who consciously try to cut calories*, and they tend not to overeat fat. However, you shouldn't *try* to eat more fat than you normally would. It's the reduced starch, not the liberalized fat, that makes people lose weight on low-carb diets. Overeating fat can stall a weight loss program. I suggest you limit yourself to average American serving sizes of meat and dairy products, with a half-portion second helping if you wish. (Typical serving sizes are listed in Appendix A.) In addition, here are some suggestions for improving the balance among the fats in your diet.

To Reduce Saturated Fat:

- Eat meat in its natural form—whole cuts of beef, pork, lamb, and poultry. Limit your consumption of processed meats like wieners, sausage, salami, and bologna.

- Cut away visible fat, preferably before cooking.
- Choose lean hamburger. Better yet, pick a lean cut of sirloin, and ask your butcher to grind it for you.
- Eat cheese mainly as an ingredient in other foods, as in salad dressings, omelets, or quiches, but avoid eating it straight, as in sliced cheese or pizza topping.
- Drink low-fat milk.
- Use margarine, preferably without partially hydrogenated oils, instead of butter.

To Increase Monounsaturated Fat:

- Whenever possible, use olive oil—preferably high-quality extra-virgin olive oil—in place of other kinds of oils, margarine, and butter.
- Eat several helpings of nuts, olives, or avocados weekly.

To Assure Adequate Omega-3 Fatty Acid:

- Eat a serving of salmon, trout, sardines, herring, or mackerel weekly.
- Eat a half cup of walnuts weekly.
- Look for free-range meats (meat from livestock that has been allowed to graze).
- Consider taking a fish oil or flaxseed supplement.

Remember, if changing the kinds of fats in your diet reduces the enjoyment you get from your low-glycemic-load eating style and causes you to eat more starch, it's probably not worth the trouble. It's important to understand that the benefits of optimizing your fat balance are largely theoretical and are dwarfed by the advantages of losing weight by any means. The changes in this chapter are worth making *only* if you're sure they won't interfere with your weight loss program.

11

Managing Cholesterol with a Low-Glycemic-Load Diet

Bill not only had high blood cholesterol but was thirty-five pounds overweight, and had signs of insulin resistance. To lower his cholesterol, he tried cutting out eggs, meat, and dairy products but found himself eating more starch and sugar. Although his cholesterol level dropped a few points, it was still too high, and he gained ten more pounds. Then his doctor prescribed cholesterol-lowering medication, which lowered his cholesterol level to normal and allowed him to go back to eating eggs, meat, and dairy products in moderation. He was then able to focus his efforts on reducing starch and sugar in his diet and relieving insulin resistance. He found it easier to lose weight, and his cholesterol level was lower than ever.

Bill typifies many patients who try to lower their blood cholesterol by going on low-cholesterol diets. They don't succeed in lowering their cholesterol levels enough to reduce their risk of heart disease much, and they end up eating more starch and sugar. Bill succeeded in losing weight and lowering cholesterol when he approached the two parts of his metabolism separately. He used medication to reduce his cholesterol level and devoted his dietary efforts to lowering his glycemic load.

Rethinking Cholesterol

It was no coincidence that the obesity rate in the United States began rising shortly after government agencies and medical organizations started warning the public about dietary cholesterol. Cholesterol fears triggered a shift in eating patterns away from eggs, meat, and dairy products toward more flour products, potatoes, and rice. Thirty years later, the lesson medical science learned—or should have learned—is that making people afraid to eat cholesterol doesn't do much to prevent heart disease but dramatically increases the risk of obesity and diabetes.

If you want to lose weight, you need to purge your thinking of the anticholesterol propaganda you've been exposed to for the past thirty years. It's not that reducing cholesterol is of itself bad. The problem is, you have to eat something, and as a practical matter, if you can't eat eggs, meat, and dairy products, you're probably going to eat more refined carbohydrates.

Is cholesterol important? You bet it is. Infiltration of arteries by cholesterol is the leading cause of death and disability of Americans and Europeans. Reducing cholesterol levels in the blood prevents heart disease more effectively than any other treatment known. The problem is that *reducing cholesterol in your food does little to reduce the cholesterol in your blood.*

Your liver makes most of the cholesterol in your body. It manufactures about three times more than you eat. If you eat less, it just makes more. Moreover, your body absorbs only about half of the cholesterol in your food. Most of it goes out in your stool. The level of cholesterol in your blood depends mainly on how efficient your system is at removing it, not on how much cholesterol you eat. High blood cholesterol is caused by genetic deficiencies of cellular receptors responsible for removing cholesterol particles from your blood, and has little to do with your diet.

Where, then, did we get the notion that dietary cholesterol causes heart attacks? In one sense, it's true: people who live in parts of the world where hunger is a constant threat have lower blood cholesterol levels and fewer heart attacks than inhabitants of wealthier countries. Short of such deprivation, however, reducing dietary cholesterol has only a modest effect on blood cholesterol. Closely supervised low-fat, low-cholesterol diets reduce blood cholesterol levels, on average, between 5 and 10 percent, which is not enough to make much of a dent in your risk of heart disease.

Keeping the Two Parts of Your Metabolism Straight

Keep in mind that the cholesterol side of your metabolism is largely independent of the carbohydrate side. How efficient your system is at removing cholesterol is determined mainly by your genes and has little to do with your diet and exercise habits. On the other hand, how well your body handles carbohydrates—how responsive it is to insulin—is *strongly* influenced by diet and exercise. In other words, your genes control the cholesterol side; your lifestyle governs the carbohydrate side.

Things that are good for the cholesterol side of your metabolism aren't necessarily good for the carbohydrate side. For example, eating less meat and fewer dairy products might lower your cholesterol level a little, but if it causes you to eat more starch and sugar, it will aggravate insulin resistance and encourage weight gain. Conversely, cutting carbs might help you lose weight but usually doesn't lower cholesterol much. To achieve a good metabolic balance, you need to manage the cholesterol and the carbohydrate parts of your body chemistry separately.

Doing Right by Your Arteries

Once you understand how cholesterol does its damage, you will see clearly what you need to do to keep your arteries healthy. Contrary to common belief, cholesterol doesn't steadily build up in arteries until they become blocked. When cholesterol particles start accumulating in artery walls, the body fights back. Defensive cells, called *macrophages*, attack these particles as if they were foreign invaders like bacteria or viruses. Normally, when macrophages encounter bacteria or viruses, they secrete enzymes called *proteinases*, which kill the intruders. Although proteinases are good for killing germs, they don't do much to cholesterol. But that doesn't deter the macrophages; they keep secreting their enzymes anyway, and that's the problem. If the battle gets intense enough, the enzymes start burning cavities in the artery wall. These cavities fill with a pasty mix of cholesterol and dead macrophages, creating soft pockets that lie under the inner lining of arteries like boils under the skin.

These cholesterol-filled pockets are what cause heart attacks. Like boils, they sometimes burst, which rips open the inner lining of the artery. The body tries to repair the tear by forming a blood clot over it, which causes more harm than good. Sometimes the clot gets so big it blocks the artery.

Now you can understand why cholesterol-lowering treatment works so well to prevent heart attacks. When you lower your blood cholesterol level, you don't just stop cholesterol from building up in your arteries; you immediately placate the macrophages that secrete the destructive enzymes responsible for damaging arteries. After a month or two, cholesterol buildup recedes, and cholesterol-filled pockets heal in with scar tissue and lose their propensity to burst.

Knowing Your Three Cholesterol Levels

Cholesterol is very sneaky. You can't tell it's getting in your arteries until the damage it does progresses to an advanced stage. That's why it's important not to wait until it causes symptoms. You need to find out if you have high blood cholesterol and correct it before it causes trouble.

You've heard that your cholesterol level should be less than 200? Forget that. Just knowing your total blood cholesterol level is not enough. You need to find out about the three different kinds of cholesterol-containing particles in your blood: bad cholesterol, good cholesterol, and triglyceride.

Bad cholesterol, called *LDL* for *low-density lipoprotein*, is the stuff that actually gets into your arteries. These particles are just the right size for seeping into artery walls and initiating the chain of events that ultimately leads to damage.

Good cholesterol, or *HDL* for *high-density lipoprotein*, does the opposite. It cleans out your arteries. These amazing particles act like vacuum cleaners. They suck up cholesterol in your artery walls and carry it back to your liver for disposal. The higher your blood HDL concentration, the better off you are. A one-point increase of your HDL level reduces your risk of heart disease as much as a three-point decrease in your LDL level.

The other cholesterol-containing particle, *triglyceride*, doesn't get into your artery walls. In fact, in the past, doctors didn't pay much attention to it. The only reason they measured it was to distinguish it from bad cholesterol. However, in recent years triglyceride has gained newfound respect. It turns out that a high triglyceride level is a reliable sign of insulin resistance. Triglyceride is actually fat traveling from your liver to your fat deposits. If you take in more carbs than your body can handle, your liver turns it to triglyceride.

Triglycerides are important for another reason. High levels deplete, or "wash away," HDL, which promotes cholesterol buildup. HDL is an important link between diet, exercise, and heart disease. Excessive dietary starch and lack of exercise aggravate insulin resistance, which raises triglyceride levels, lowers HDL, and increases the risk of heart disease.

Determining if You Have a Cholesterol Problem

To estimate your risk of developing artery disease, you need to consider not only your bad and good cholesterol levels but also your age, blood pressure, family history, and whether you smoke or have diabetes. The National Cholesterol Education Program has developed a simple method for determining whether you have a cholesterol problem.

First, you need to call your doctor and find out your LDL, HDL, and triglyceride levels. Some pharmacies also will measure these for you. Then answer the following questions, and add up the points:

Question	Points
Are you a male forty-five years of age or older or a female fifty-five years of age or older?	Yes = 1; No = 0
Do you smoke cigarettes?	Yes = 1; No = 0
Do you have an immediate family member who has had a heart attack before age sixty-five?	Yes = 1; No = 0
Do you have high blood pressure, or are you being treated for high blood pressure?	Yes = 1; No = 0
Is your HDL level 40 or less if you are a male, or 50 or less if you are a female?	Yes = 1; No = 0
Is your HDL level 60 or greater?	If yes, subtract a point

Total Points _____

The more of these risk points you have, the lower your LDL level should be to offset the risk. Here's how to tell what your LDL level should be:

- If your score is 0 or 1, your LDL level should be lower than 160.
- If your score is 2 or more, your LDL level should be less than 130.
- If you have diabetes, your LDL should be lower than 100.
- If you already have artery narrowing or blockage, you should aim for an LDL of 70 or less.

Crafting a Cholesterol Strategy

If you're overweight but your LDL level is safely within the normal range, you can focus your attention on reducing your glycemic load and not worry about cholesterol. However, if according to the National Cholesterol Education Program guidelines you need to lower your LDL level, you have two options. You can try to lower it by changing your diet, or you can take cholesterol-lowering medication.

Lowering Cholesterol by Changing Your Diet

If you are overweight *and* you have a high LDL level, the first step in changing your diet should be to reduce your intake of starch and sugar. "Wait a minute," you might be thinking, "shouldn't I be on a low-cholesterol diet?" To lose weight, you have to cut out starch and sugar anyway, so you might as well see if that lowers your cholesterol. Often it does, especially for people with severe insulin resistance. However, if eliminating starch and sugar doesn't bring your cholesterol down, you can try to reduce your intake of saturated fat and cholesterol in addition to cutting out starch and sugar. (For tips on reducing saturated fat and cholesterol, see Chapter 10.)

The problem with trying to cut out fat and cholesterol as well as starch and sugar is that it leaves you little else to eat. You might think you have the willpower to do it, but it's hard to cut out bread, potatoes, rice, and sweets in addition to avoiding eggs, meat, and dairy products. Most people can't tolerate such deprivation for long. It's also not a very effective way to lower cholesterol. Low-fat, low-cholesterol diets just don't reduce blood cholesterol levels enough to have much of an effect on most people's risk of heart disease.

Cholesterol-Lowering Medications

The easiest, most effective way to lower cholesterol is to face the fact that you have a genetic quirk in your cholesterol metabolism and take a cholesterol-lowering medication. One pill a day of a *statin*-type of cholesterol-lowering medication (such as Mevacor, Pravachol, Lescol, Zocor, Lipitor, Crestor, or Vytorin) counteracts the genetic defect that causes high blood cholesterol and allows your body to process it normally. You can then return to eating eggs, meat, and dairy products in moderation and focus your dietary efforts on eliminating starch and sugar—the culprits that most likely caused you to gain weight.

Statin medications are truly miracle drugs. They have saved more lives than any medication ever developed. Instead of lowering cholesterol a few percentage points, which is all that low-cholesterol diets can usually achieve, statins drop blood cholesterol levels by 40 or 50 percent. Within days, the macrophages in your arteries stop secreting their destructive enzymes, and damaged arteries begin to heal. After a few months, cholesterol buildup recedes, and narrowed arteries often open back up. One cholesterol-lowering pill a day can reduce the risk of heart disease by as much as 67 percent.

A low-glycemic-load diet is a perfect complement to cholesterol-lowering medication. Research shows that when people taking statins switch from a low-*cholesterol* to a low-glycemic-load diet, even if they eat more fat and cholesterol, their cholesterol balance improves. If you take a statin, you can usually go back to eating eggs, meat, and dairy products in moderation. This makes it easier to eliminate refined carbohydrates, which relieves insulin resistance, promotes weight loss, and raises HDL—good cholesterol. The easiest and most effective way to lose weight *and* lower bad cholesterol, then, is to focus your dietary and exercise efforts on the carbohydrate side of your metabolism and let medication take care of the cholesterol side.

12

Rebalancing Your Metabolism

J udy was fifty pounds overweight. She knew she needed to reduce her intake of bread, potatoes, and rice to lose weight, and she had been told since childhood that sweets are bad. She liked eggs, meat, and dairy products but had heard that these are full of cholesterol. She had also read that salt and caffeine could cause high blood pressure. It seemed there was little she *could* eat.

Judy typifies many patients I talk to these days whose efforts to lose weight are hindered by too many dietary distractions. Judy needed to rearrange her priorities to take care of what was most important. The risk to her health posed by her weight dwarfed any threat from dietary cholesterol, sugar, salt, or caffeine.

Avoiding Distractions

We tend to overestimate our ability to change our diet and our exercise habits. Then, when we fall short of our expectations, we get disheartened and quit. The trick to losing weight is to make sure the demands you place on yourself fall within your capabilities. That means focusing on what's throwing your body chemistry out of kilter and on nothing else.

There would be little harm in eliminating cholesterol, sugar, salt, and caffeine if it didn't interfere with your efforts to lose weight. The problem is that cutting out so many things leaves too little to enjoy. Face it: if you attempt to change too much, you will probably tire of the joylessness of the routine and go back to your old ways.

If your blood cholesterol level is OK, there's really no point in trying to avoid dietary cholesterol. Even if your cholesterol is high, cutting out cholesterol-containing foods doesn't help much. In fact, it often works against you, because you usually end up eating more starch and sugar. Besides, if you truly have a cholesterol problem, keeping your level down is too important for you to rely on diet. As I discussed in Chapter 11, you're usually better off taking cholesterol-lowering medication.

As for salt and caffeine, avoiding them won't prevent high blood pressure. Short of medications, the best way to keep your blood pressure down is to keep your weight down. In fact, the most important lifestyle change you can make for your health in general is to focus your efforts on losing weight and avoid being distracted by other dietary concerns.

Focusing on What Caused You to Gain Weight

You've learned that being overweight is not a manifestation of a weak willpower or a self-indulgent personality. It's the result of a hormonal imbalance brought on by the convergence of the following three conditions:

- **A genetic muscle problem:** You were born with a quirk in your slow-twitch muscle fibers that causes them to fall into a deeper-than-normal dormant state when you don't use them.
- **Long periods of inactivity:** The twentieth century lulled you into thinking—as it did most of us—that it's physiologically normal to go for days without walking

more than a few hundred feet at a time. Consequently, your slow-twitch muscle fibers spend too much time turned off to insulin, and your pancreas has to make more insulin than normal to handle the carbohydrates in your diet.

- **Too much starch and sugar:** Economic forces and misdirected fears about cholesterol have driven up the starch and sugar content of your diet to levels your insulin-resistant body can't handle. Repeated glucose shocks make your pancreas secrete huge amounts of insulin, which distorts your appetite and encourages your body to store calories as fat. In addition, starch short-circuits into your bloodstream in the first foot or two of your intestine and never reaches the last part of your digestive tract, where important appetite-suppressing hormones come from.

So how do you put your body chemistry back in balance? You can't change your genes, but genetic quirk or not, you can restore your muscles' sensitivity to insulin, and you can reduce the number of glucose shocks in your diet.

Most folks know that exercise promotes weight loss and that starch and sugar are fattening, but often people make the mistake of paying too much attention to one aspect of their metabolism and not enough to another. They might succeed in reducing their glycemic load but fail to activate their slow-twitch muscle fibers. Or they might exercise regularly but continue to assail their bodies with glucose shocks.

You can lose weight by lowering your glycemic load or by sensitizing your muscles to insulin, but the easiest way is to do both. Athletes talk about being in "the zone" or finding "the sweet spot" where they perform their best. If you eliminate the major dietary offenders and do just enough of the right kind of exercise, your metabolism will enter a "zone" where it performs best. Your insulin levels will drop like a rock, and without deprivation or strenuous exercise, your body chemistry will start working with you instead of against you.

Taking Inventory

To know where best to apply your effort, you need to take a close look at the state of your body chemistry. This section will help you answer the following questions:

- How much is your weight affecting your health?
- How insulin resistant are you?
- How much time do your slow-twitch muscle fibers spend in the sleep mode?
- What is the glycemic load of your diet?
- Do you have high blood cholesterol?

Knowing what aspects of your body chemistry are abnormal will help you put your metabolism back in balance with as little effort and disruption of your life as possible.

How Much Is Your Weight Affecting Your Health?

From the standpoint of appearance, the definition of overweight depends on personal preference and the fashion of the day; but what you need to know is how much your weight is affecting your metabolism. Excess weight triggers a vicious cycle: it worsens insulin resistance, and insulin resistance, in turn, promotes more weight gain. The more overweight you are, the worse your insulin resistance, and the more you need to focus on relieving it.

A good way to judge how much your weight is affecting your metabolism is to look at statistics relating body weight to diseases caused by insulin resistance such as diabetes and heart disease. Scientists have devised a formula for judging risk using height and weight measurements. They call it the *body mass index (BMI)*. To estimate your risk, first find your BMI in Table 12.1 by looking at your height and weight.

Regardless of your gender, most nutritionists regard a BMI of 24 or less as being ideal, 25 to 29 as mildly overweight, 30 to 34 as markedly overweight, and 35 or greater as obese. Once you know your BMI, you can use Figure 12.1 to determine your risk of obesity-related diseases.

Table 12.1 Body Mass Index Table

BMI	Normal		Moderately Overweight					Markedly Overweight					Obese					
	23	24	25	26	27	28	29	30	31	32	33	34	35	36	37	38	39	40
								Body Weight (pounds)										
58	110	115	119	124	129	134	138	143	148	153	158	162	167	172	177	181	186	191
59	114	119	124	128	133	138	143	148	153	158	163	168	173	178	183	188	193	198
60	118	123	128	133	138	143	148	153	158	163	168	174	179	184	189	194	199	204
61	122	127	132	137	143	148	153	158	164	169	174	180	185	190	195	201	206	211
62	126	131	136	142	147	153	158	164	169	175	180	186	191	196	202	207	213	218
63	130	135	141	146	152	158	163	169	175	180	186	191	197	203	208	214	220	225
64	134	140	145	151	157	163	169	174	180	186	192	197	204	209	215	221	227	232
65	138	144	150	156	162	168	174	180	186	192	198	204	210	216	222	228	234	240
66	142	148	155	161	167	173	179	186	192	198	204	210	216	223	229	235	241	247
67	146	153	159	166	172	178	185	191	198	204	211	217	223	230	236	242	249	255
68	151	158	164	171	177	184	190	197	203	210	216	223	230	236	243	249	256	262
69	155	162	169	176	182	189	196	203	209	216	223	230	236	243	250	257	263	270
70	160	167	174	181	188	195	202	209	216	222	229	236	243	250	257	264	271	278
71	165	172	179	186	193	200	208	215	222	229	236	243	250	257	265	272	279	286
72	169	177	184	191	199	206	213	221	228	235	242	250	258	265	272	279	287	294
73	174	182	189	197	204	212	219	227	235	242	250	257	265	272	280	288	295	302
74	179	186	194	202	210	218	225	233	241	249	256	264	272	280	287	295	303	311
75	184	192	200	208	216	224	232	240	248	256	264	272	279	287	295	303	311	319
76	189	197	205	213	221	230	238	246	254	263	271	279	287	295	304	312	320	328

Height (inches) applies to the leftmost BMI/height column (values 58–76).

Source: National Heart, Lung, and Blood Institute (nhlbi.nih.gov/guidelines/obesity)

As you can see, the more you weigh, the higher your risk of diabetes and heart disease. Notice that if your BMI is less than 25, the effect of a few extra pounds is negligible. The risk starts rising above 25, and beyond 30, it skyrockets. The higher your BMI, the more critical it is that you lose weight and the more you need to focus your efforts on improving the carbohydrate side of your metabolism.

How Insulin Resistant Are You?

Some overweight individuals have worse insulin resistance than others do. An amazingly simple yet accurate way to estimate the

Figure 12.1 Cardiovascular Risk Grows with Body Mass Index

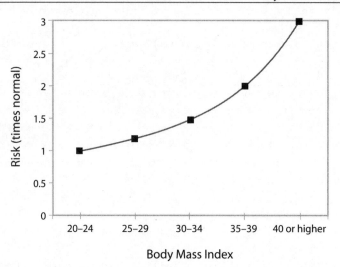

Source: Modified from Bray, G. A. 1992. Pathophysiology of obesity. *American Journal of Clinical Nutrition* 55:488S

severity of your insulin resistance is to measure your abdominal circumference at the level of your navel. (*Note*: Use a tape measure. Do not rely on pants size.)

- Regardless of your height, if your girth measured at your navel is more than thirty-eight inches if you're a male or thirty-four inches if you're a female, your risk of diabetes *doubles*.
- If your girth is more than forty inches if you're a male or thirty-six inches if you're a female, your risk *triples*.
- If your girth is more than forty-two inches if you're a male or thirty-eight inches if you're a female, your risk *quadruples*.

The good news is that the worse your insulin resistance, the more dramatically it will improve when you correct the factors that cause it. If you concentrate on reducing your glycemic load and activating your slow-twitch muscle fibers, your body shape will quickly change. Your abdomen will shrink before the rest of you does. In fact, the best way to monitor your progress in reversing insulin resistance is not to follow your weight, since you might gain muscle as you lose fat. Just notice the way your pants fit.

How Much Time Do Your Slow-Twitch Muscle Fibers Spend in the Sleep Mode?

As I discussed in Chapter 8, it takes twenty to thirty minutes of aerobic activity like walking or jogging to get your slow-twitch muscles to wake up and start responding to insulin. After a few hours, they slowly start losing sensitivity; in forty-eight hours, they're back where they started. Thus, the more time you spend going longer than forty-eight hours without exercise, the more time your body spends in an insulin-resistant state.

More than a day or two a week of insulin resistance will raise your risk of obesity and diabetes. That means to eliminate insulin resistance periods, you need to exercise at least *every other day*— that's four times a week at regular intervals. Research studies consistently show that this is the frequency of exercise needed to lose weight and prevent diabetes. However, if you have a low fidget factor (for example, if you spend more than six hours a day in front of a computer or a television screen), you should probably exercise as many days in a week as you spend engaged in sedentary activities.

What Is the Glycemic Load of Your Diet?

You can gauge how much insulin your body has to make by adding up the glycemic loads of the foods you eat. According to research linking diet with cardiovascular disease, most people can handle a glycemic load of approximately 500 a day or less without harmful insulin excess. A daily tally greater than 500 will drive up your insulin levels and promote weight gain.

As I mentioned in Chapter 4, you usually don't need a list of glycemic-load ratings of foods to tell if your glycemic load is too high. Only a handful of refined carbohydrates are usually responsible: bread, potatoes, rice, breakfast cereal, pasta, and sugar-containing soft drinks. More than one average-size serving of one of these foods a day, when added to the smaller glycemic loads you get in other foods, is usually enough to push your glycemic load above 500. More than three full servings a day of starch will definitely promote weight gain and increase your risk of diabetes and heart disease.

Do You Have High Blood Cholesterol?

High blood cholesterol is a silent killer. It causes no symptoms until it reaches an advanced stage. You can be thin and physically fit but still have a dangerously high cholesterol level. As you learned in Chapter 11, the only way to tell if you have a problem is to measure the levels of the three different kinds of cholesterol particles in your blood. If, according to the National Cholesterol Education Program guidelines, your bad cholesterol level is too high, you probably have a genetic quirk in your body's mechanisms for removing cholesterol. This can only mean trouble. In addition to losing weight, you need to find a fail-safe means of keeping your blood cholesterol level down.

You've learned that the way your body handles carbs and its ability to remove cholesterol from your blood are two separate aspects of your metabolism. How your body metabolizes carbohydrates depends largely on your diet and physical activity patterns. Your cholesterol level depends on how efficient your system is at removing cholesterol, and your genes determine this. The easiest and most effective way to put your body chemistry back in balance is to use medications if necessary to lower cholesterol, and devote your dietary and exercise efforts toward relieving insulin resistance.

Relieving Insulin Resistance: The Rewards

If you do what you need to do to allieve insulin resistance—eliminate glucose shocks and activate your slow-twitch muscle fibers—even if you don't try to cut calories, remarkable things will happen:

- **You can usually lose weight without dieting.** Eliminating the dietary culprits that cause your body to produce too much insulin removes little in the way of richness and flavor from your diet. You can eat satisfying amounts of good food and still lose weight.
- **You reduce your risk of diabetes.** When you reduce the amount of insulin your pancreas has to make, you reduce your risk of type 2 diabetes.
- **If you have type 2 diabetes, it will improve dramatically.** If you combine standard medication for type 2 diabetes with the program described in this book, chances are your blood glucose levels will return to normal. (*Caution*: If you are already taking medication for diabetes, the dosages needed might decline significantly, causing your blood glucose levels to fall too low. You should monitor your blood glucose closely and discuss your treatment with your doctor.)
- **Your cholesterol profile will improve.** Although relieving insulin resistance usually doesn't reduce bad cholesterol levels much, it dramatically lowers blood triglyceride levels and raises the concentrations of protective cholesterol, HDL, in your blood. This improves the balance between good and bad cholesterol and reduces your risk of heart and blood vessel disease.
- **Your mood will improve.** Improving the way your body handles carbohydrates will soften the adrenaline fluctuations that jerk your nerves back and forth from being jangled to burned out. Your mood, concentration, and energy levels will improve noticeably.
- **You might notice you sleep better.** There is a strong correlation between insulin resistance and irregular breathing at night, which disturbs the quality of sleep. If you keep your insulin resistance in check and lose a few pounds, you might snore less, sleep better, and be wider awake during the day.
- **If you have polycystic ovary syndrome (PCOS), it will improve.** Insulin resistance causes polycystic ovary

syndrome, the most common cause of menstrual irregularity and infertility. Relieving insulin resistance often restores normal ovulation. When women with PCOS stop eating starch and start exercising, they often start menstruating regularly and get pregnant.

Freedom from Dieting

Crash dieters often experience a sense of impending disappointment, as if they expect their house of cards to come tumbling down at any time, which in fact, it usually does. It's a different story for people who understand insulin resistance and do what they need to do to relieve it. They exude the confidence of someone who gets it. They have a clear vision of what they are trying to accomplish, and they know the difference between what they can change and what they cannot.

Losing weight by reducing the glycemic load of your diet and targeting physical activity toward sensitizing your muscles to insulin bears little resemblance to the timeworn approach of starving yourself and sweating off pounds. As you will see in the next chapter of this book—where you'll find great ideas for meals and delicious recipes—you can eat heartily, feel satisfied, and reduce your glycemic load. Add enough of the right kind of exercise to turn on your slow-twitch muscle fibers, and you will discover the key to a healthier way of living you can continue for life.

13

Low-Glycemic-Load Meals and Recipes

few years ago, I discovered I had a reason to reduce my own glycemic load. I had diabetes. My initial reaction was one of dismay. I thought my fine-dining days were over. I soon came to realize I was wrong.

Back when we were told we should cut down on fat and cholesterol, I loved everything that was supposed to be bad for you: steaks, chops, cheeses, cream sauces, omelets, avocados, and nuts. I followed the party line and tried to avoid them. However, by the time I developed diabetes, it was becoming apparent that these foods were not as bad as everyone thought. They really weren't what caused high blood cholesterol, and they didn't raise blood sugar. I discovered I could enjoy them in abundance, and my blood cholesterol levels were lower than ever. All I had to do was concentrate on carbohydrates.

A More Exciting Way to Eat

Initially, cutting out carbs looked like a big job, but once I became familiar with the concept of glycemic load, I realized there were only a handful of carbohydrates I needed to cut out: grain products, potatoes, rice, and soft drinks. I could even enjoy sweets in moderation, as long as they weren't starchy ones.

I also discovered there's a bonus to reducing your glycemic load: when you stop eating bread, potatoes, and rice with every meal, you make room for more variety and flavor. Truthfully, I eat heartier now than I did before.

Of course, if someone tells you that you shouldn't eat something, you start thinking you can't live without it. But honestly, is starch so wonderful you're willing to sacrifice your health and your looks for it? Bread, potatoes, and rice are "comfort foods." Because they were the first foods our mothers fed us, they presumably evoke feelings of warmth and security. But humans have no biological need for starch and no natural craving for it. Getting the tasteless paste out of your diet makes room for healthier food and more exciting tastes and textures.

So forget about depriving yourself. Consider this as an opportunity to broaden your palate and embark upon a culinary adventure. Here are some suggestions to help you get started:

- **Don't throw away your old cookbooks.** The day after I told my wife I had diabetes, she made a trip to the bookstore to buy diabetic cookbooks. Later, we realized there's no need to invest in special cookbooks to follow a low-glycemic-load diet. Virtually all of the cookbooks she already had offered a wealth of starch-free dishes. If you don't own a cookbook, forget about diet cookbooks. Make your first purchase a classic like *The Joy of Cooking* or *The Silver Palate Cookbook*.
- **Learn how to recognize starch in recipes.** Spotting starch is simple. It's always visible and rarely blended with other ingredients. Look for recipes that contain no crusts, breading, potatoes, or rice. A tablespoon or two of flour or a half cup of bread crumbs to hold other ingredients together won't hurt. Neither should a few teaspoons of sugar in an otherwise starch-free dish. Just avoid large hunks of starch.
- **Remember that "low carb" is not the same as "low glycemic load."** Most of the recipes in low-carb

cookbooks are fine. However, some of these books go too far in eliminating fruits, vegetables, milk products, and sugar but not far enough in getting rid of starch. Some purportedly low-carb recipes contain significant amounts of ingredients you should avoid, such as whole-grain flour and brown rice. Although these less refined starches contain more vitamins and fiber than their whiter versions do, they're just as bad when it comes to causing glucose shocks.

Molly Siple, nutrition editor of *Natural Health* magazine, a registered dietitian, and author of several popular cookbooks, has provided a couple dozen of her favorite recipes, which capture the spirit of the low-glycemic-load style of eating. Try some of them, or even just read about them, and you'll see that reducing your glycemic load can be the key to a richer, more enjoyable way of eating.

Of course, all you have to do is look around you to find good low-glycemic-load recipes. I am fortunate to live in a town with wonderful regional cuisine and some great cooks. Kathy Casey, author of *Pacific Northwest: The Beautiful Cookbook* and *Dishing with Kathy Casey*, contributed a few of her favorite low-glycemic-load recipes. Duke Moscrip, owner of Duke's Chowder House restaurants and winner of several awards for his chowders, provided a couple of great low-glycemic-load chowder recipes. My wife, a great cook, also added a few of our favorite dishes. You will find, however, that there's really no need for special food preparation to follow a low-glycemic-load eating style. In each food category, I have listed several classic dishes you can easily find in most cookbooks and frequently on restaurant menus.

Breakfast Dishes

Finding good low-glycemic-load breakfasts is often a challenge. Many of us start the day with a glucose shock caused by cereal or baked goods. In this section, you'll find some great low-glycemic-load suggestions.

- **Omelets:** It's been scientifically proven that if you begin the day with an omelet, you will eat fewer calories for the rest of the day than if you start out with a breakfast cereal. Learn to make an omelet, and you have the key to a delicious breakfast that won't raise your blood sugar. You can add cheese, onions, mushrooms, peppers, or meat. They all have low glycemic loads.
- **Eggs with bacon, ham, or sausage:** In the old days when we were paranoid about cholesterol, we used to joke about how bad bacon and eggs are for you. But the truth is, these foods are a better way to start the day than eating breakfast cereal or buns.
- **All-Bran:** All-Bran is undoubtedly the best way of assuring adequate insoluble fiber. If it gets a little monotonous, you can liven it up by eating it with yogurt instead of milk, throwing in a spoonful or two of some other kind of cereal, or adding some fruit.
- **Fruit and yogurt:** Plain yogurt is a good low-glycemic-load food that sticks to your ribs. Unfortunately, commercially sweetened yogurts are packed with sugar. Buy plain yogurt (don't bother with fat-free), add some fruit, and sweeten to taste with a half teaspoon of sugar or artificial sweetener.
- **Fruit and cottage cheese:** Fruit and cottage cheese combine to make a quick low-glycemic-load standard that should keep you satisfied until lunch. Again, don't bother with the low-fat kind.

Homemade Breakfast Burrito

Too busy to cook a hot breakfast? Make a batch of these fast-food favorites on Sunday, keep them in the refrigerator, and microwave them during the week before rushing off in the morning. They'll stick to your ribs all day. The trick is to reduce the glycemic load by using low-carb tortillas. The following recipe gives you the basics, but feel free to add fresh cilantro, sour cream, and lime juice.

6 ounces prepared pork sausage
¼ cup chopped onion
½ teaspoon chili powder
4 eggs
4 high-fiber, reduced-carb wheat tortillas
4 ounces cream cheese, cut into bits, or grated
    cheddar cheese
1 medium tomato, seeded and chopped
Salt and freshly ground pepper
Salsa, optional

1. Crumble the sausage into a skillet. Add the onion and chili powder. Mix together, and cook over medium heat, stirring occasionally, until meat is thoroughly cooked and the sausage and onion begin to brown, about 10 minutes. Transfer to a bowl, and keep warm.

2. Scramble the eggs. Pour into the skillet used for cooking the sausage mixture. Cook the eggs, stirring frequently, just until the eggs are no longer runny, 2 to 4 minutes. Remove the pan from the heat.

3. Meanwhile, sprinkle each tortilla with a few drops of water, stack on a plate, and cover with a paper towel. Microwave 30 seconds.

4. To assemble the burritos, lay the warm tortillas on serving plates. Divide the sausage mixture equally, making a band of filling across the middle of each

tortilla. Top with equal portions of scrambled eggs, cheese, and tomato. Season with salt and pepper.

5. Fold one side of the tortilla over the filling, and then the other. Turn the burrito over to keep the burrito closed. Garnish with salsa if desired.

Note: To make them ahead of time, assemble the burrito with all the ingredients except the tomato, which is more difficult to keep fresh. Wrap the burrito in plastic wrap, and refrigerate. To reheat, remove the plastic wrap, and microwave the burrito 1 minute. Serve topped with the fresh tomato.

Serves 4

Nutrition information: Per serving: 448 calories, 66% fat (32.7 g; 13.1 g saturated), 15% carbs (17.0 g), 19% protein (20.7 g), 281 mg cholesterol, 7.6 g fiber, 1,028 mg sodium

Colorful Herb Frittata

The orange carrots, along with the green herbs, make for a festive dish. The carrots add substance—replacing the starchy potato, which is a standard part of the usual frittata. This baked form of scrambled eggs takes well to so many different flavorings, from cooked ham, sausage, and smoked fish to mushrooms, sun-dried tomatoes, and cheese. Frittatas also keep well refrigerated, so you can eat a slice at a time over two or three days for a quick, gourmet breakfast.

> 1 medium carrot, peeled and cut crosswise into 2-inch
> lengths
> 3 sprigs fresh dill
> 3 sprigs fresh parsley
> 2 green onions, trimmed
> 6 eggs
> 1 teaspoon Dijon mustard
> Salt
> 2 tablespoons extra-virgin olive oil
> Sour cream for garnish

1. Preheat the oven to 350°F.

2. Boil the carrots in a small pot over medium-high heat until tender, about 10 minutes.

3. Meanwhile, remove the stems from the dill and parsley. Finely chop the two herbs. Slice the green onions crosswise ¼ inch thick. Dice the carrots.

4. Break the eggs into a medium-size bowl, and add the mustard. Beat the eggs with a fork. Mix the herbs, onions, and carrots into the eggs. Season with salt.

5. Put the oil in a medium to large ovenproof skillet, preferably nonstick, over medium heat. When the oil is hot, pour the egg mixture into the skillet, and reduce the

heat to medium-low. Cook, undisturbed, until the bottom of the frittata is firm, about 7 minutes.

6. Transfer the skillet to the oven. Be careful not to grab the skillet handle when hot.

7. Bake the frittata just until the top is runny. Check for doneness after 10 minutes. Cook for another 5 minutes or so, but be very careful not to overcook.

8. Using an oven mitt, remove the skillet from the oven, and place it on a work surface. Use a spatula to loosen the frittata from the pan. Tip the skillet, and slide the frittata gently onto a serving platter. Serve immediately, or refrigerate to enjoy chilled. Garnish with sour cream.

Serves 6

Nutrition information: Per serving: 134 calories, 66% fat (9.8 g; 2.6 g saturated), 12% carbs (4.2 g), 22% protein (7.2 g), 215 mg cholesterol, 0.9 g fiber, 348 mg sodium

High-Fiber Bran Muffins

Most commercial bran muffins fall short when it comes to fiber, and because of their high flour content, they have unacceptable glycemic loads. However, you can make your own bran muffins with the fiber content increased enough to do you some good. You can also reduce the glycemic load by substituting almond meal for whole wheat flour. For variety, you can add apple chunks, blueberries, or cranberries; substitute walnut oil for some of the safflower oil; use toasted almonds or walnuts; or spice with grated fresh gingerroot. These handy muffins deliver over 10 grams of fiber each, as much as a bowl of All-Bran cereal.

> 1½ cups All-Bran cereal
> 1 cup whole almonds or whole wheat flour
> 3 cups wheat bran
> 3 tablespoons whole wheat flour if using almond meal
> ⅓ cup dark brown sugar
> 1 teaspoon baking powder
> 1 teaspoon baking soda
> 2 teaspoons allspice
> 1 teaspoon cinnamon
> ½ teaspoon nutmeg
> ½ teaspoon salt
> ½ cup apple chunks, blueberries, or cranberries
> 3 eggs
> 1¼ cups milk
> ½ cup unrefined safflower oil
> 1 teaspoon vanilla extract
> Butter for greasing muffin cups

1. Adjust oven rack to lower-middle position. Preheat oven to 350°F.

2. In a food processor with a metal blade, process the All-Bran until it has the texture of bread crumbs. Transfer to

a large bowl. If using almond meal instead of flour, process the almonds until they have the texture of cornmeal.

3. Add the almonds (or flour) to the bowl along with the wheat bran, sugar, flour, baking powder, baking soda, allspice, cinnamon, nutmeg, and salt. Stir to combine ingredients. Add fruit or nuts, if desired.

4. Break the eggs into another large bowl, and lightly beat with a fork. Add the milk, oil, and vanilla. Whisk to combine thoroughly.

5. Add about one-third of the dry ingredients to the egg-milk mixture and mix thoroughly. Repeat until all the ingredients are used.

6. Coat the muffin tin cups lightly with butter. Spoon the batter into the muffin tin cups, which will be filled to the rim. Bake until a toothpick inserted into the center of one of the muffins comes out clean or with a few moist particles adhering to it, about 20 minutes. Remove from the oven, and cool slightly on a wire rack, about 5 minutes. Remove the muffins from the tin, and serve warm.

Makes 12 muffins

Nutrition information: Per serving: 231 calories, 48% fat (14.4 g; 1.8 g saturated), 39% carbs (26.5 g), 13% protein (8.1 g), 39 mg cholesterol, 10.5 g fiber, 280 mg sodium

Chipotle Deviled Eggs

(From Dishing *by Kathy Casey)*

"This spicy twist on an old favorite became a huge hit and must be among my most requested recipes ever."—Kathy Casey

> 1 dozen eggs
> 3 tablespoons regular or low-fat sour cream
> 3 tablespoons mayonnaise
> ½ teaspoon salt
> ½ teaspoon Dijon mustard, optional
> 1 to 2 tablespoons chipotle puree (see Note)
> 1 teaspoon minced garlic
> 2 tablespoons very thinly sliced green onion

> *Topping*
> ½ cup diced (¼-inch) tomatoes
> 1 tablespoon minced white onion
> 2 tablespoons minced fresh cilantro
> 1 to 2 teaspoons chipotle puree (see Note)

1. Place the eggs in a saucepan, and cover with cool water to 1 inch above the eggs. Bring to a boil over medium-high heat, and then simmer 10 minutes. Remove the eggs from the heat, and run cool water over them. When they are cool, carefully peel them under running water.

2. Cut the eggs in half lengthwise, and remove the yolks to a mixing bowl. Set the egg white halves on a platter; cover and refrigerate.

3. Mash the egg yolks to a smooth consistency with a fork or potato masher. Mix in the sour cream, mayonnaise, salt, mustard, 1 to 2 tablespoons chipotle puree, and garlic until smooth. (You can also do this in a mixing bowl with a whip attachment.) Stir in the green onions.

4. Spoon the yolk mixture into a pastry bag fitted with a plain or large star tip, and then squeeze (pipe) the mixture evenly into the egg white halves.

5. To make the topping, in a small bowl, mix together tomatoes, onion, cilantro, and chipotle puree. Top each egg half with 1 teaspoon of the tomato mixture.

Note: To make chipotle puree, place contents of 1 can of chipotle peppers in adobo sauce (found in the Mexican foods section of well-stocked supermarkets) in a blender or food processor, and puree until smooth. Freeze any remaining puree for another use, such as spicing up ketchup or barbecue sauce.

Serves 6

Nutrition information: Per serving: 220 calories, 70% fat (17.1 g; 4.9 g saturated), 6% carbs (3.1 g), 25% protein (13.1 g), 432 mg cholesterol, 0.4 g fiber, 511 mg sodium

Breakfast Cereal Sundae

Commercial flavored yogurts are loaded with sugar to appeal to the palates of fourteen-year-olds. However, you can easily make your own with much less sugar, starting with unsweetened yogurt and adding flavorings like cinnamon, vanilla, strawberries, blueberries, mango, or fresh mint and sweetening to taste with a half-teaspoon or so of sugar. You can also layer the yogurt with cereal and fruit. A nectarine was chosen for this recipe because these come to market sweet and juicy almost year-round and taste almost like peaches. Serve this concoction in an ice-cream sundae glass or a large, stemmed wine or water glass, and you'll be starting the day with a nutritious, high-fiber dessert.

> **1 sprig mint**
> **½ cup yogurt**
> **½ cup All-Bran cereal**
> **1 ripe nectarine, sliced**
> **Berries for garnish, optional**

1. Chop the mint leaves, and put in a small bowl along with the yogurt. Stir to combine.

2. Put ⅓ of the All-Bran into the bottom of an ice-cream sundae glass. Top with ⅓ of the yogurt and a couple of nectarine slices.

3. Repeat this layering sequence twice, using up all the ingredients.

4. For your "cherry on top," top the sundae with a few raspberries or a strawberry, and sit down to breakfast.

Serves 1

Nutrition information: Per serving: 226 calories, 19% fat (5.7 g; 2.8 g saturated), 66% carbs (45.4 g), 15% protein (9.4 g), 16 mg cholesterol, 12.7 g fiber, 133 mg sodium

Salads

Salads don't have to be low-calorie rabbit food. Greens and oils complement rich ingredients like meat, cheese, nuts, avocados, and olives beautifully; and the glycemic loads of most salads are negligible. When you start a meal with a salad, the fiber slows the absorption of whatever glucose you get in the rest of your food. And there's no law that says salads have to fit on a small plate. You can make a meal of a hearty salad. Here are some popular low-glycemic-load salads you'll often find in cookbooks and restaurant menus, followed by some of my favorite recipes:

- **Cobb salad:** This American classic combines romaine or any leaf lettuce with cubes of cooked chicken, tomato, bacon, crumbled blue cheese, avocado, and chopped egg. It's usually served with a vinaigrette or blue cheese dressing.
- **Taco salad:** This Tex-Mex favorite is simply taco fillings on a plate. Lettuce, tomato, avocado, and onion are combined with shredded beef or chicken and flavored with taco seasoning topped with shredded cheddar cheese, salsa, and a dollop of sour cream.
- **Chop salad:** The ingredients of this salad are finely chopped to the same size to blend their tastes. It includes romaine lettuce, tomatoes, green peppers, and green onions paired with diced Italian salami, mozzarella cheese, smoked turkey, and garbanzo beans and thoroughly tossed with vinaigrette dressing.
- **Tomato and mozzarella salad:** The Italians call this salad *caprese*—slices of tomato topped with slices of fresh mozzarella, sprinkled with slivers of fresh basil, and drizzled with olive oil—a special treat in the summertime, when delicious tomatoes and fresh basil are available.
- **Greek salad:** This tasty classic salad includes tomato, cucumber, onion, marinated artichoke hearts, kalamata olives—sometimes lettuce, sometimes not—and chunks of feta cheese tossed with olive oil.

- **Caesar salad:** This one needs no introduction; it has become so popular that you'll find it on most menus. Combine romaine lettuce, Caesar dressing with or without anchovies, and shredded Parmesan cheese, and if you like, top with shrimp or chicken.

Hearty Steak and Mushroom Salad

Dining on this salad is like eating a steak dinner (which it is), made with a sizable portion of flank steak, plus grilled mushrooms and a topping of crumbled blue cheese. Prep time is just 15 minutes, and cooking takes 10 minutes. The recipe makes one serving for times when you are cooking for yourself. For more, just multiply the ingredient amounts by the number of people dining.

> 1 2-inch length of cucumber, peeled
> ⅓ cup roasted sweet red pepper (see Note)
> 2 cups chopped romaine lettuce
> 3 large button mushrooms, trimmed
> 2 tablespoons extra-virgin olive oil
> 2 teaspoons balsamic vinegar
> Salt and freshly ground black pepper
> 4 ounces beef round steak or London broil
> 2 tablespoons crumbled blue cheese

1. Cut the cucumber crosswise in thick slices, and halve the slices. Put the cucumber, red pepper, and lettuce in a large bowl. Quarter the mushrooms, and set them aside.

2. In a small bowl, mix together the oil and vinegar with a fork. Drizzle over the vegetables, and toss. Season with salt and pepper.

3. Heat a ridged griddle pan or skillet over medium-high heat. Add the steak and the mushrooms to the pan. Cook the steak to medium-rare, 4 to 5 minutes per side. While the steak cooks, occasionally turn the mushrooms, so they cook evenly.

4. Transfer the steak to a cutting board, and cut the meat across the grain into thin slices.

5. To assemble the salad, pile the dressed lettuce and vegetables on a dinner plate. Top with the slices of steak and mushrooms. Scatter the cheese over the meat. Serve immediately, perhaps with a glass of red wine.

Note: Grill a fresh sweet red pepper, or use the tasty ones sold in glass jars in most supermarkets.

Serves 1

Nutrition information: Per serving: 585 calories, 66% fat (43.9 g; 11.8 g saturated), 7% carbs (10.2 g), 27% protein (39.1 g), 89 mg cholesterol, 3.8 g fiber, 916 mg sodium

Salad Niçoise

Instead of potato, this version of the classic niçoise uses an array of complementary flavors including, if desired, a piquant onion relish (see next recipe). It comes together as an arranged plate of colorful vegetables with reds, yellows, greens, and rosy purple. Serve it with ripe Brie or Camembert, or for variety, make it with fresh tuna steak or salmon.

½ pound fresh green beans, trimmed
2 eggs
2 (6-ounce) cans tuna, packed in water, drained
1 bell pepper, preferably yellow or red
4 cups romaine lettuce, chopped into thin strips
2 tablespoons chopped fresh basil
1 tablespoon capers
6 tablespoons extra-virgin olive oil
2 tablespoons balsamic vinegar
1 teaspoon Dijon mustard
Salt and freshly ground black pepper
8 cherry tomatoes, halved
8 olives, preferably niçoise or kalamata
Molly's Piquant Onion Relish, optional
8 anchovies

1. Steam green beans for 10 minutes until al dente and still bright green.

2. Boil the eggs 10 to 12 minutes, so the yolks are pleasantly creamy, or 15 minutes if you want them cooked through. Plunge the eggs into cold running water for 2 minutes, and gently remove the peel. Quarter the eggs, and set them aside.

3. Put the tuna, bell pepper, romaine, basil, and capers in a large bowl, and toss to combine.

4. To make the dressing, put the oil in a small bowl, and add the vinegar, mustard, salt, and black pepper. Stir vigorously, and pour over the tuna mixture.

5. Divide the salad equally on four dinner plates. Distribute the beans, eggs, tomatoes, and olives, making a cluster of each around the edge of the salad. Garnish the green beans with a spoonful of onion relish, if desired (see following recipe), and top each serving with 2 anchovies.

Serves 4

Nutrition information: Per serving: 355 calories, 70% fat (28.9 g; 4.2 g saturated), 13% carbs (12.5 g), 16% protein (14.7 g), 34 mg cholesterol, 5.4 g fiber, 2,136 mg sodium

Molly's Piquant Onion Relish

This savory onion relish enlivens grilled meats, especially chicken and pork. It's also a great complement to the Salad Niçoise recipe.

> **1 red onion, peeled and sliced thin**
> **½ cup apple cider vinegar**
> **½ cup water**
> **2 cloves garlic**
> **1 bay leaf**
> **½ teaspoon thyme**
> **½ teaspoon rosemary**
> **Salt and freshly ground pepper**

1. Soak the onion slices in water for 10 minutes, and drain.

2. Put the onions, vinegar, ½ cup water, garlic, bay leaf, thyme, and rosemary in a saucepan. Bring to a boil, reduce heat to medium, and cook 10 minutes, stirring occasionally. Allow to cool. Season with salt and pepper.

Serves 8

Nutrition information: Per serving: 18 calories, 3% fat (0.1 g; 0.0 g saturated), 87% carbs (4.6 g), 10% protein (0.5 g), 0 mg cholesterol, 0.7 g fiber, 2 mg sodium

Green Peppercorn Chicken Salad

This spicy, unusual variation of chicken salad is one of my favorite dishes. It gets better after it sits in the refrigerator for a few days, so it's a great make-ahead dish. You can serve it over a bed of greens with tomato wedges, blanched green beans, and imported kalamata olives on the side.

> 3 to 4 medium cloves garlic
> 1 cup olive oil
> 2 tablespoons green peppercorns, packed in brine,
>   rinsed and drained
> 2 tablespoons lemon juice
> 1 teaspoon sherry wine vinegar
> 1 teaspoon fines herbes
> ½ teaspoon salt
> ½ teaspoon red pepper flakes
> ½ teaspoon coarsely ground black pepper
> 2 pounds boneless, skinless chicken breasts

1. Place the garlic and ½ cup olive oil in a food processor, and process until the garlic is finely chopped. Pour into a large mixing bowl.

2. Add the remaining ½ cup of oil and the peppercorns, lemon juice, vinegar, fines herbes, salt, red pepper flakes, and black pepper to the chopped garlic, whisking until all ingredients are combined.

3. Place the chicken in a large pan, and add enough water to cover. Place the pan over medium heat, bring liquid to a simmer, and cook 5 minutes. Turn chicken, and cook for another 5 minutes, until the juices of the chicken run clear when pierced with a fork.

4. Remove the chicken from the pan, place it on a cutting board, and cut it across the grain into bite-size pieces. Add the chicken immediately to the olive oil mixture.

5. When the poaching liquid has cooled, strain it, and add ⅓ cup to the chicken mixture. Toss well to coat.

Serves 6

Nutrition information: Per serving: 494 calories, 68% fat (37.8 g; 5.4 g saturated), 2% carbs (2.8 g), 29% protein (35.3 g), 88 mg cholesterol, 0.7 g fiber, 418 mg sodium

Warm Sweet and Sour Pork Salad

In Thai cooking, salads can be a main course made with all sorts of vegetables and fresh herbs topped with meats and shrimp hot from the grill. Sample this salad made with marinated pork and dressed in a spicy Thai chili sauce, and it's sure to become a favorite dinnertime meal. You don't have to wait to go to a Thai restaurant to enjoy the tangy flavors of Thai cuisine. But a word of warning: Thai cooking typically goes heavy on the fiery chiles. Tune the spiciness to your own taste.

Marinade
3 cloves garlic, minced
1 1-inch-length gingerroot, peeled and minced
2 tablespoons fish sauce
2 tablespoons soy sauce

Salad
1 pound boneless loin of pork
4 sprigs cilantro, stems removed
1 scallion, trimmed
4 cups chopped iceberg lettuce
1 cucumber, peeled
1 mango, peeled
1 avocado, peeled, cut in half, and seed removed
1 tablespoon spicy Thai chili sauce, such as Thai
    Kitchen brand, or to taste
¼ cup lime juice
4 small red or green chiles, or to taste, seeds removed
    and finely chopped
4 tablespoons roasted peanuts

1. To make the marinade, in a small bowl, mix the garlic, ginger, fish sauce, and soy sauce.

2. Cut the pork into thin slices, and cut these into strips. If necessary, cut the strips in half so they are about 1½ to

2 inches long. Put the pork strips in a shallow dish, and add the marinade. Toss to coat the meat, cover, and refrigerate 1 hour.

3. Meanwhile, finely chop the cilantro, and cut the scallion crosswise into ¼-inch slices. Put in a large bowl, along with the lettuce. Toss to combine.

4. Cut the cucumber crosswise into quarters and each quarter vertically into sticks. Cut slices of mango crosswise into smaller wedges. Cut each avocado half into slices.

5. Distribute the lettuce mixture equally on four dinner plates. Arrange equal amounts of cucumber, mango, and avocado on each bed of lettuce.

6. Mix the chili sauce, lime juice, chiles (if desired), and ¼ cup water in a small bowl. Set aside.

7. Stir-fry the pork and marinade in a skillet for 3 to 4 minutes, until the pork is no longer pink.

8. Pour the chili sauce and lime juice mixture into the skillet, and stir with the meat. Once the sauce is heated, spoon the pork onto each salad. Scatter peanuts over each salad, and serve immediately.

Serves 4

Nutrition information: Per serving: 476 calories, 49% fat (26.5 g; 5.9 g saturated), 17% carbs (21.5 g), 34% protein (39.8 g), 93 mg cholesterol, 6.8 g fiber, 359 mg sodium

Beet and Pear Salad with Warm Breaded Goat Cheese

The small amount of flour in this recipe bonds the goat cheese as it melts into a creamy morsel that perfectly complements the sweet and tart flavors of the dish. Enjoy this salad topped with toasted walnuts.

> 1 6-ounce log goat cheese, chilled
> 3 tablespoons flour
> 1 egg, lightly beaten
> 1 tablespoon milk
> ⅓ cup plain bread crumbs
> Salt and freshly ground pepper
> ¼ cup walnut oil
> 2 tablespoons sherry wine vinegar
> 1 teaspoon Dijon mustard
> 1 shallot, peeled and minced
> ¼ teaspoon thyme
> 1 large cooked beet or 1 15-ounce can sliced beets, drained
> 1 ripe Anjou pear
> 4 cups mâche, mesclun, or other tender, delicately flavored lettuce
> ¼ cup extra-virgin olive oil

1. Cut the chilled goat cheese log crosswise into eight even rounds.

2. Put the flour in a shallow dish. In a small bowl, whisk together the egg and milk. Put the bread crumbs in a separate shallow dish. Season the goat cheese rounds with salt and pepper. Dredge one round in flour, shaking off the excess, dip in the egg wash, and then dredge in the bread crumbs, pressing to coat it well. Repeat with the remaining rounds. Return the rounds to the refrigerator to chill 30 minutes.

3. To prepare the salad dressing, put the walnut oil, vinegar, mustard, shallots, and thyme in a small bowl, and whisk to combine.

4. Peel and quarter the beet, and cut it into thin wedges. Core the pear, and cut it into slim slices. Put the lettuce in a large bowl. Add the beet and pear, and drizzle with the salad dressing. Gently toss. Distribute on four salad plates, placing a few of the beet and pear slices on top of the lettuce as a garnish.

5. Put the olive oil in a small sauté pan over medium-high heat. Carefully place the goat cheese rounds into the hot oil, taking care not to crowd the pan. Cook the cheese 1 to 2 minutes, until the bread crumbs on the underside are lightly browned; turn with a spatula. Cook an additional 1 to 2 minutes until the cheese has softened. Transfer two slices to each of the salad plates, and serve immediately.

Serves 4 as starter course, 2 as main course

Nutrition information: Per serving as a starter course: 367 calories, 65% fat (11.4 g; 8.1 g saturated), 23% carbs (21.8 g), 12% protein (11.4 g), 33 mg cholesterol, 3.0 g fiber, 281 mg sodium

Parmesan Crisps

If you want something crunchy in your salad, try these lacy wafers of Parmesan cheese instead of croutons. They're a snap to make, and you can keep them in your refrigerator for future use. The baking sheet liner in this recipe prevents the crisps from sticking—a very handy kitchen aid.

> **8 tablespoons Parmesan cheese**
> **Special equipment: nonstick silicone half-sheet pan liner such as Silpat**

1. Preheat the oven to 500°F. Lay the nonstick liner on a baking sheet.

2. Scoop a tablespoon of Parmesan cheese on the liner. Repeat to fill the baking sheet, making two rows of four mounds each. Press on each mound with the back of a spoon, and spread until small gaps appear in the cheese. This will create a lacy pattern when baked.

3. Bake 3 to 4 minutes, until melted and golden. Remove from oven, and allow the crisps to cool 5 minutes, until firm enough to transfer with a spatula to a wire rack. Serve immediately, or refrigerate in an airtight container.

Serves 4

Nutrition information: Per serving: 57 calories, 59% fat (3.7 g; 2.4 g saturated), 3% carbs (0.5 g), 38% protein (5.2 g), 10 mg cholesterol, 0.0 g fiber, 231 mg sodium

Molly's Chicken Tonnato Salad

The Italians invented a surprisingly pleasant combination of flavors called *vitello tonnato*. It's a fish sauce served over cold sliced veal. You can also use this tart but smooth sauce to enliven a poached chicken breast, either alone or as part of a salad with marinated artichokes and fresh basil. The combination makes an elegant lunch or a satisfying meal on a hot summer's evening.

Sauce and Chicken
4 boneless, skinless chicken breast halves (about 1 pound)
½ cup mayonnaise
1 (6-ounce) can chunk light tuna, packed in water, drained
3 anchovies
1 tablespoon capers
1 tablespoon lemon juice
Freshly ground pepper

Salad
4 cups washed salad greens that include arugula
1 (15-ounce) can cannellini beans, rinsed
1 (6-ounce) jar marinated artichoke hearts, drained
3 tablespoons extra-virgin olive oil
1 tablespoon balsamic vinegar
10 large basil leaves, chopped
1 clove garlic, peeled and minced
Salt and freshly ground pepper
4 wedges fresh lemon

1. Put the chicken breasts in a pot with enough water to cover. Poach over medium heat, about 15 minutes (until inside is no longer pink). Allow to cool in the water.

2. To make the sauce, put the mayonnaise, tuna, anchovies, capers, and lemon juice in a food processor with a metal

blade. Process until blended but not smooth. Season with pepper.

3. Put the salad greens, beans, and artichoke hearts in a large bowl.

4. Whisk together the olive oil, vinegar, basil, and garlic in a small bowl. Season to taste with salt and pepper. Drizzle over the salad, and toss to combine flavors.

5. Thinly slice the chicken breasts, and distribute them among four dinner plates, arranging them to leave room for the salad. Spoon about 3 tablespoons of tuna sauce over each serving of chicken. Place the salad next to the chicken, and serve with a wedge of lemon.

Serves 4

Nutrition information: Per serving: 567 calories, 45% fat (28.9 g; 3.8 g saturated), 16% carbs (23.9 g), 38% protein (52.9 g), 122 mg cholesterol, 7.3 g fiber, 1,075 mg sodium

Soups and Chowders

A bowl of soup is a great way to begin a meal, and most have low glycemic loads. Some hearty soups are filling enough to have as a main dish. Here are some popular low-glycemic-load soups you'll see in cookbooks and restaurant menus, followed by a recipe for one of my favorites:

- **Gazpacho:** This chilled summertime favorite is made with tomatoes, bell peppers, onions, and cucumbers.
- **Borscht:** The Russian classic has many variations, made with beets, beef, tomatoes, onions, cabbage, and seasonings. It's delicious hot or chilled topped with a dollop of sour cream.
- **Hot and sour soup:** Chances are, you'll find this bracing soup with pork, mushrooms, and tofu on the menu in your favorite Chinese restaurant or in many cookbooks.
- **Garden vegetable:** You can make this nutritious favorite with chicken, beef, or vegetable broth and all kinds of vegetables; just pluck out the potatoes.
- **Bouillabaisse:** This French favorite is a hearty fish soup that combines shellfish, fish fillets, bacon, and vegetables.

Sweet Red Pepper Soup
Topped with Sour Cream

Red pepper soup is mainstream gourmet when flavored with summer savory but suddenly becomes Mexican gourmet when you add oregano. Either way, be sure to garnish the warm soup with chilled sour cream to add richness and balance the textures and flavors.

> 1 cup finely chopped onion
> 1 tablespoon unrefined safflower oil
> 1 (15-ounce) jar roasted yellow and red peppers, or
>   1 yellow and 1 red fresh bell pepper, roasted,
>   trimmed, and chopped
> 1 medium tomato
> 2 cups chicken broth
> ¼ teaspoon dried summer savory
> Salt and freshly ground black pepper
> Sour cream for garnish

1. In a small skillet, sauté the onion in the oil over medium heat until softened and translucent, about 5 minutes.

2. Put the roasted peppers, tomato, and onion in a food processor fitted with a metal blade. Puree with a splash of the chicken broth.

3. Transfer the puree to a saucepan. Add the rest of the broth and the summer savory. Season with salt and black pepper.

4. Bring the soup almost to a boil, and reduce heat to low. Cover the pot, and simmer 15 minutes. Ladle the soup into individual bowls, and garnish each serving with a dollop of sour cream.

Serves 4

Nutrition information: Per serving: 129 calories, 50% fat (7.5 g; 2.3 g saturated), 36% carbs (12.3 g), 14% protein (4.5 g), 6 mg cholesterol, 2.2 g fiber, 402 mg sodium

Duke's Water Chestnut Clam Chowder

(Courtesy of Duke Moscrip)

Every Seattleite knows where Duke's Chowder House is. Duke Moscrip has been making chowders and winning prizes for them since the Space Needle went up. I was blown away by this low-glycemic-load chowder. You won't believe how good clam chowder is when it's made with water chestnuts instead of potatoes.

¼ cup diced bacon
¼ cup butter
¼ cup diced onion
¼ cup diced celery
1 medium-size clove garlic, chopped
¼ cup water
2 tablespoons clam base
½ cup heavy whipping cream (unsweetened)
½ cup chopped water chestnuts (⅜-inch cubes)
1 tablespoon cornstarch or ThickenThin not/Starch thickener (a starchless substitute for cornstarch)
¼ teaspoon white pepper
½ teaspoon black pepper
¼ teaspoon basil
¼ teaspoon fresh chopped parsley
¼ teaspoon thyme
1 bay leaf
¼ teaspoon marjoram
¼ teaspoon dill
¾ cup clam juice
12 ounces canned clams, drained and chopped

1. Place the bacon in a heavy kettle, and cook on medium heat until it has lost its transparency (or is about halfway done).

2. Add the butter, onion, celery, and garlic, and cook until the onion becomes translucent.

3. In a separate container, combine the water and clam base, and mix until the clam base is completely dissolved. Add to the bacon and vegetable mixture.

4. Add the cream, water chestnuts, thickener, white and black pepper, basil, parsley, thyme, bay leaf, marjoram, dill, and clam juice, and heat to 180°F. Be careful not to scorch the cream; it's best to leave heat on medium.

5. Add the clams at the end, since they are already cooked. (If you put them in too early, they can become tough.)

Note: If you live in an area that has good fresh clams, you may substitute them for the canned chopped clams; allow about 16 clams per person. Steam them in wine or low-carb beer, shuck them, and add them to the chowder just before serving. Wow your guests by leaving a few in the shell, and garnish the bowl with fresh clams and chopped parsley and other herbs.

Serves 4

Nutrition information: Per serving: 455 calories, 52% fat (26.9 g; 15.1 g saturated), 23% carbs (27.2 g), 24% protein (27.2 g), 133 mg cholesterol, 1.7 g fiber, 418 mg sodium

Duke's Low-Carb Butternut Squash and Shrimp Chowder

(Courtesy of Duke Moscrip)

This is another one of Duke's home runs. The squash seems to pick up the flavor of the shrimp, and the pepper and curry give it some zip.

> 1 large butternut squash
> 2 tablespoons butter
> ¼ cup diced celery
> ¼ cup diced onion
> 1 tablespoon chopped garlic
> 1 teaspoon dried basil
> 1 tablespoon shrimp base
> 1 teaspoon curry powder
> 1 tablespoon Old Bay seasoning
> 1 tablespoon fresh chopped parsley
> 1 teaspoon fresh cracked black pepper
> ½ cup heavy whipping cream (unsweetened)
> Pinch of kosher salt
> 1½ cups whole milk
> 1⅓ pounds fresh large shrimp, cooked
> 1 roasted red bell pepper, julienned

1. Preheat oven to 350°F. Cut the butternut squash in half, and remove seeds, leaving the outside skin on. Place the squash, skin side down, in a roasting pan. Add ¼ cup water to the pan, and cover. Roast the squash 45 minutes. Cool in the refrigerator. After the squash is cool, scoop it from the shell. Dice squash into ¼-inch cubes, and reserve them until the chowder is done. You can do this step a day in advance.

2. In a heavy pot, melt the butter, and sauté the celery, onion, garlic, and basil until the onion and celery become translucent.

3. In a bowl, combine the shrimp base, curry powder, Old Bay seasoning, parsley, black pepper, cream, salt, milk, and shrimp. (Reserve some shrimp for garnish.) Mix well. Add to the ingredients in the pot, and heat to 180°F over medium heat.

4. When the chowder is hot, add the squash, reserving several pieces for garnish.

5. Ladle the chowder into large bowls, and garnish with fresh shrimp, roasted red bell pepper, and a piece of the butternut squash.

Note: You can make the chowder base and serve it up to three days later. Reheat over medium heat to avoid scorching.

Serves 4

Nutrition information: Per serving: 415 calories, 26% fat (10.7 g; 6.0 g saturated), 33% carbs (31.1 g), 41% protein (37.4 g), 325 mg cholesterol, 4.9 g fiber, 461 mg sodium

Red Meat Dishes

Red meat got some bad press in the old days when we were told it causes high blood cholesterol. Although we know now that meat is not the problem, along the way you might have lost interest in learning about new ways to prepare it. Chances are, your meat dishes have remained somewhat unimaginative over the years. Of course, a grilled steak with nothing but salt and pepper for seasoning will always be a favorite, but there are many exciting ways to enhance the flavor and texture of meat. You can also experiment with dry rubs, marinades, flavored butters, glazes, salsas, and classic sauces like Madeira and béarnaise. Here are some popular ways of enhancing meat dishes, followed by several of my favorite meat recipes:

- **Boeuf bourguignonne:** The classic French version of braised beef stew is prepared with bacon, mushrooms, carrots, pearl onions, and red wine. It's a winter favorite.
- **London broil:** This is flank steak quickly grilled or broiled over high heat and thinly sliced across the grain. Experiment with different marinades, and throw leftovers into a salad with lettuce, mushrooms, red onion, and crumbled blue cheese.
- **Meat loaf:** A family favorite in American homes for decades, this is comfort food without the carbs (except for an inconsequential amount of bread crumbs).
- **Chili:** This spicy mix of beef and seasonings made from chili peppers originated in Texas, but options for preparing it extend far beyond the original "con carne" version. You can make it with any kind of meat or poultry.
- **Kabobs:** Thread meat, poultry, or fish onto skewers, alternating with pieces of vegetable. Brush with olive oil or marinade, and grill.
- **Barbecue:** Now beloved by Americans in all parts of the country, barbecue dishes can be made in the oven or on

the grill in endless ways, including beef brisket, country-style pork ribs, and chicken slathered in your favorite sauce.

- **Curries:** Experiment with this exotic import for a different, delicious taste sensation. There are endless varieties; you can make curry with lamb, chicken, shrimp, or vegetables. The flavors will be so intriguing, you won't miss eating the rice that often accompanies it.

Savory Greek Lamb Shanks and Green Beans

The robust flavorings of this dish are decidedly Greek, thanks to the marinated olives, oregano, cinnamon, and garlic. Instead of the traditional roasted potatoes, this lamb is paired with super-garlicky lima beans, creating a robust meal that would satisfy Zorba.

> 2 tablespoons extra-virgin olive oil
> 4 lamb shanks, about 1 pound each, trimmed of excess fat
> Salt and pepper, to taste
> 1 medium onion, sliced (2 cups)
> 5 cloves garlic, minced
> ½ teaspoon oregano
> 2 teaspoons cinnamon
> ½ cup red wine or chicken stock
> 1 (15-ounce) can tomatoes, drained
> Zest of ½ small lemon
> ½ cup marinated black or green olives
> 1 (10-ounce) package frozen baby lima beans
> 1 tablespoon chopped fresh parsley

1. Heat 1 tablespoon of the oil in a deep skillet or casserole with a tight-fitting lid. Add the lamb shanks, and cook

about 10 minutes over medium-high heat, browning on all sides and seasoning with salt and pepper. Transfer the meat to a platter.

2. Pour off all but 2 tablespoons of fat from the skillet. Add the onion, and cook over medium heat about 10 minutes, stirring occasionally until soft and golden. Stir in 2 cloves garlic, the oregano, and the cinnamon, and cook another minute.

3. Add the wine, tomatoes, and lemon zest and stir to mix. Return the lamb to the skillet, turning it in the sauce to coat it on all sides. Cover, and cook on low heat 30 minutes.

4. Turn over the lamb shanks, add the olives and 3 cloves of garlic, and cover the skillet. Cook another 30 minutes. Add the lima beans, making sure they are completely covered with sauce, adding wine if necessary. Continue cooking the lamb mixture until the meat is very tender and nearly falling off the bone, about 1 hour.

5. Place the lamb shanks on each dinner plate, along with a generous amount of the cooking sauce and beans. Sprinkle with the parsley. For a feast, add a Greek salad topped with feta cheese.

Serves 4

Nutrition information: Per serving: 484 calories, 32% fat (16.7 g; 4.7 g saturated), 26% carbs (30.4 g), 42% protein (48.0 g), 126 mg cholesterol, 8.5 g fiber, 410 mg sodium

Mexican Pot Roast with Chili Powder Rub

Rubs are dry marinades—a great way to infuse an ordinary piece of meat with extraordinary flavor. In this recipe, chili powder is combined with garlic, oregano, and cinnamon to produce a dish with a decidedly south-of-the-border flavor. Serve with pinto beans, guacamole, and some chilled beer.

> 1 tablespoon chili powder
> 1 teaspoon dried oregano
> ½ teaspoon cinnamon
> 2 cloves garlic, minced
> Salt and freshly ground pepper to taste
> 2 pounds chuck or rump roast
> 2 medium onions, sliced (4 cups)
> 1 carrot, chopped (1 cup)
> 1 stalk celery, chopped (1 cup)
> ½ cup red wine
> ½ cup homemade chicken, beef, or vegetable stock, or
>   water

1. In a small bowl, combine the chili powder, oregano, cinnamon, garlic, salt, and pepper.

2. Sprinkle the spice mixture all over the roast, and rub it into the meat. Refrigerate, covered, overnight.

3. Heat the oil over medium-high heat in a heavy pot with a tight-fitting lid. Put the meat in the pot and brown on all sides, about 10 minutes total.

4. Meanwhile, slice the onions, and chop the carrot and celery into uniform small pieces.

5. Transfer the meat to a platter. Transfer the vegetables to the pot, and cook over medium-high heat, stirring frequently, until softened and beginning to brown, about 10 minutes.

6. Add the red wine, and cook until most of the wine has evaporated. Scrape the bottom of the pot with a wooden spoon to prevent the vegetables from sticking.

7. Add the stock, and return the meat to the pot. Cover the pot, and reduce the heat to very low. Cook the roast, turning occasionally, until very tender, 2 to 2½ hours, until a fork can easily pierce the meat and the juices run clear. Take care not to overcook the meat.

8. Transfer the roast to a serving platter, and keep it warm. Skim the fat from the juices in the pot. Cook the juices, along with the mass of softened vegetables, on high, stirring and scraping the pot, until the juices reduce to a thick liquid. Slice the meat, and serve the pot roast with the sauce and vegetables. This dish also makes an excellent leftover.

Serves 7

Nutrition information: Per serving: 351 calories, 33% fat (12.5 g; 4.5 g saturated), 12% carbs (10.4 g), 55% protein (44.6 g), 131 mg cholesterol, 2.8 g fiber, 178 mg sodium

Tenderloin of Pork with Citrus Salsa

Tenderloin is free of bones and easy to handle and slice into tidy servings. Its only drawback is that it is not, on its own, the most flavorful of cuts. However, this recipe remedies that. The meat is treated to a spice rub and served with a dazzling, sweet-tart-piquant fruit salsa!

Salsa
2 navel oranges, peeled, seeds removed, separated into
    segments, and cut into chunks
½ cup diced red onion
Juice of 2 limes (4 tablespoons)
1 tablespoon chopped fresh cilantro
1 teaspoon minced fresh chili pepper, or to taste
1 clove garlic, minced
1 teaspoon cumin
¼ teaspoon chili powder
Salt and freshly ground black pepper to taste

Rub
1 teaspoon chili powder
½ teaspoon cumin
½ teaspoon dry mustard
½ teaspoon sage
½ teaspoon salt
⅛ teaspoon cayenne

1 tablespoon extra-virgin olive oil, plus extra for the
    baking pan
1 (1½- to 2-pound) pork tenderloin, in one piece

1. For the salsa, put the oranges, onion, lime juice, cilantro, chili pepper, garlic, cumin, and chili powder in a bowl. Mix thoroughly. Season with salt and pepper. Cover and chill in refrigerator.

2. For the rub, combine the chili powder, cumin, mustard, sage, salt, and cayenne in a small bowl. Rub the meat all over with this mixture.

3. Preheat the oven to 500°F. Lightly oil a baking pan.

4. Heat the oil in a large skillet until hot but not smoking. Add the pork, and sear each side 2 to 3 minutes.

5. Place the meat in the oiled pan, and bake until almost cooked through but still slightly pink in the very center, about 10 to 15 minutes. The meat is done when an instant-read thermometer inserted into the very center of the tenderloin reads 145°F. Let the tenderloin rest for 10 minutes, so it will retain juices when you carve it.

6. Cut into ½-inch-thick slices, and serve with the citrus salsa.

Serves 6

Nutrition information: Per serving: 227 calories, 37% fat (9.2 g; 3.3 g saturated), 13% carbs (7.4 g), 51% protein (27.7 g), 76 mg cholesterol, 1.3 g fiber, 55 mg sodium

Buffalo Burgers Stuffed with Cheddar Cheese

Just for a change, rustle up some buffalo meat. It's similar in flavor to beef but with slightly gamey overtones. In addition, free-range buffalo, like wild game, is a source of valuable omega-3 fatty acids. These burgers are sure to become a favorite around your household.

> 4 (4-ounce) lean buffalo patties (see Note)
> ½ cup finely chopped onion
> ¼ cup chopped fresh parsley
> 2 teaspoons Worcestershire sauce
> Salt and freshly ground pepper, to taste
> 1 cup loosely packed grated sharp cheddar cheese
> Pickle relish, optional
> 4 low-carb tortillas, optional

1. Put the buffalo meat, onion, parsley, Worcestershire sauce, salt, and pepper in a large bowl, and mix together.

2. Divide the meat into 4 equal portions. Shape each into a ball. Poke a deep hole into each ball, manually or with a spoon handle. Fill each with a quarter of the cheese. Press some meat over the opening to encase the cheese. With a spatula, flatten each ball into a patty ¾ inch thick.

3. Warm a grill pan over medium-high heat, and cook the patties about 5 minutes on each side for medium doneness.

4. Serve immediately, garnished with tart pickle relish or vinaigrette coleslaw. You can also fold the patty into a low-carb tortilla, and add the usual hamburger toppings.

Note: Buffalo meat patties are available frozen, and butchers can order select cuts from one of the growing number of producers.

Serves 4

Nutrition information: Per serving: 264 calories, 36% fat (10.4 g; 5.2 g saturated), 3% carbs (2.2 g), 61% protein (38.1 g), 111 mg cholesterol, 0.5 g fiber, 376 mg sodium

Sunday Slow-Cooked Roast Beef

(From Dishing *by Kathy Casey)*

"Wow! The half bottle of wine, 20 cloves of garlic, and thickened pan juices make the sexiest, tastiest roast beef gravy ever."
—Kathy Casey

> 1 (3- to 3½-pound) beef chuck roast
> 2 tablespoons vegetable oil
> 1 tablespoon kosher salt
> ½ teaspoon pepper
> 1 large onion, peeled and cut into eight wedges
> 1½ cups sliced mushrooms
> ½ bottle (about 1½ cups) red wine
> 3 tablespoons flour
> 20 cloves garlic, peeled
> 5 sprigs fresh thyme
> 4 carrots, cut into 1½-inch pieces
> 4 stalks celery, cut into 1½-inch pieces
> 1 tablespoon chopped fresh basil, optional

1. Preheat oven to 325°F.

2. With paper towels, pat the roast dry. Heat the oil in a large ovenproof Dutch oven over high heat until hot.

3. Rub the roast with the salt and pepper. Place the beef in the hot pan, and sear on all sides until well browned. Remove the meat to a platter. Transfer the onion wedges and mushrooms to the pan, and stir for a few minutes. Tuck the roast back into the pan, pulling the onion and mushroom mixture up from under the roast.

4. Whisk together the wine and flour until smooth, and add to the roasting pan, along with the garlic and thyme. Bring to a simmer, and then cover the pan and transfer the roast to the oven.

5. Roast about 2 hours. Add the carrots and celery, and continue to roast for ½ hour to 1 hour, or until the meat is fork-tender.

6. Stir the basil into the sauce.

7. Cut the roast into thick slices or large chunks, depending on your preference, and serve with the sauce drizzled over it.

Note: If the sauce is not thick enough, make a cornstarch slurry using 1 tablespoon cornstarch mixed with 2 tablespoons water. Whisk the slurry into the simmering sauce, a little at a time, until the desired thickness is reached.

Serves 6

Nutrition information: Per serving: 647 calories, 32% fat (21.6 g; 7.7 g saturated), 14% carbs (21.9 g), 54% protein (78.7 g), 229 mg cholesterol, 5.0 g fiber, 2,189 mg sodium

Roasted Pork Loin with Fennel Spice Rub

(From Dishing *by Kathy Casey)*

With this recipe, the roasted pork pan juices and drippings stirred with sour cream make for a delicious sauce accompaniment, enhanced by the great flavor combination of fennel and orange.

> *Rub*
> 1 (2½-pound) boneless pork top loin roast, tied
> 1 tablespoon fennel seed, crushed well
> 2 tablespoons orange zest
> 2 tablespoons dried thyme
> ¼ teaspoon dried red pepper flakes
> 1 large shallot, peeled and quartered
> 2 teaspoons kosher salt
> 1 tablespoon Dijon mustard
> 2 tablespoons olive oil
>
> *Sauce*
> ¼ cup plus 2 tablespoons water
> ½ cup wine
> 1½ cups sour cream
> 1½ teaspoons cornstarch

1. Preheat the oven to 350°F. Place a rack in a shallow roasting pan. Pat the pork roast dry with paper towels.

2. In a food processor, combine the rub ingredients, and process until finely chopped. Smear the pork on all sides with the rub, being sure to use it all. For more intense flavor penetration, rub the roast up to 4 hours before cooking.

3. Place the roast on the rack in the roasting pan, and cook 1½ to 1¾ hours or until a meat thermometer inserted into the center registers 160°F.

4. Remove the roast from the pan to a platter to rest for 10 minutes before carving while you make the sauce.

5. Place the hot roasting pan on a burner, and add ¼ cup water and the wine, scraping up all the pan drippings from the bottom of the pan. Bring to a boil, then reduce to a simmer, and whisk in the sour cream.

6. Whisk together the cornstarch and 2 tablespoons water in a small cup, and then whisk it into the sauce. Cook until the sauce is thickened and has come to a boil. Remove from the heat. Thinly slice the pork, and serve with the sauce.

Chef's tip: The rub is also wonderful smeared on pork chops before grilling or on a whole chicken before roasting.

Serves 6 to 8

Nutrition information for 6 servings: Per serving: 581 calories, 56% fat (34.8 g; 14.7 g saturated), 3% carbs (4.7 g), 41% protein (56.2 g), 178 mg cholesterol, 0.1 g fiber, 1,444 mg sodium

Chicken Dishes

Chicken has become a mainstay of the American diet because it is less expensive than other main-course options and endlessly versatile. It can be served hot or cold and prepared in dozens of different ways.

- **Coq au vin:** This French classic is a chicken stew slowly simmered with mushrooms, onions, garlic, herbs, and red wine until the meat falls away from the bone.
- **Chicken fricassee:** This delicate, creamy dish combines chicken and vegetables—a longtime favorite on American dinner tables.
- **Chicken parmigiana:** This Italian-American dish combines *lightly* breaded chicken cutlets with tomato sauce and Parmesan and mozzarella cheeses. (Substitute eggplant for chicken for a vegetarian version of this dish.)

Roasted Chicken with Vegetable Gratin

This basic French bistro fare has simple flavors brilliantly combined. The chicken thighs stay moist—baked slowly in the oven—and broiling the vegetables gives them a rich, chewy crust of Parmesan cheese.

¼ teaspoon salt
¼ teaspoon pepper
⅛ teaspoon grated whole nutmeg
8 skinless, boneless chicken thighs (about 1½ pounds)
1 clove garlic, halved
1 pound zucchini, trimmed
1 (14.5-ounce) can diced tomatoes, preferably Glen Muir organic tomatoes
½ teaspoon dried thyme
2 tablespoons extra-virgin olive oil

½ cup grated Parmesan cheese
Juice of half a lemon
1 tablespoon chopped fresh parsley

1. Preheat the oven to 350°F. Oil a shallow baking dish.

2. Combine the salt, pepper, and nutmeg in a small bowl.
   Sprinkle the seasoning mixture evenly on the chicken.
   Place the chicken in the prepared baking dish. Cover
   with foil, and set aside.

3. Rub the bottom of a large baking dish (about 10″ × 14″)
   with the garlic. Cut the zucchini crosswise into ⅜-inch
   slices. Arrange the slices in the baking dish, laying them
   flat. Pour the tomatoes over the zucchini, and sprinkle
   the thyme and olive oil over the vegetables.

4. Bake the chicken and vegetables 30 minutes. Remove the
   chicken from the oven, turn the chicken over, and return
   it to the oven to bake uncovered for 30 more minutes.

5. Remove both dishes from the oven and turn on the
   broiler. Sprinkle the cheese over the vegetables and
   return them to the oven. Broil for 3 or 4 minutes, until
   the cheese melts and browns.

6. Meanwhile, transfer the chicken to a serving platter, and
   garnish with a squeeze of lemon juice and the chopped
   parsley.

7. To serve, bring the gratin dish of vegetables and the
   platter of chicken to the table for guests to help
   themselves. Finish the meal with a green salad and fresh
   berries with a bit of whipped cream.

Serves 4

Nutrition information: Per serving: 542 calories, 46% fat (27.8
g; 7.8 g saturated), 13% carbs (18.0 g), 41% protein (54.6 g),
170 mg cholesterol, 3.2 g fiber, 1,112 mg sodium

Chicken Divan

This traditional recipe—which pairs chicken and broccoli—originally called for a white sauce made with butter, flour, and milk. Over the years, the homemade white sauce has been replaced with ingredients that can be purchased off the shelf, making it quick and easy to assemble. There are many different recipes for chicken divan. This one was handed down to my wife from her mother. The recipe serves 6 to 8, but it can easily be halved for a small family or doubled to serve a crowd.

> 2 packages frozen broccoli or a couple of generous crowns of fresh broccoli
> 3 to 4 pounds poached chicken breast
> 2 cans condensed low-sodium cream of chicken soup
> 1 cup mayonnaise
> 1 teaspoon curry powder
> 1 tablespoon dry sherry
> 1 cup shredded cheddar cheese

1. Preheat oven to 350°F. Lightly coat a large baking dish with cooking spray.

2. Line the bottom of the dish with broccoli spears and generous bite-sized pieces of chicken breast.

3. Combine the condensed soup, mayonnaise, curry powder, sherry, and ½ cup of the cheese in a large bowl. Pour over the broccoli and chicken. Top with the remaining ½ cup cheese.

4. Bake 20 to 30 minutes until the cheese has melted and the sauce is bubbly.

Serves 6 to 8

Nutrition information for 6 servings: Per serving: 845 calories, 52% fat (49.3 g; 12.8 g saturated), 8% carbs (16.3 g), 40% protein (41.0 g), 247 mg cholesterol, 4.8 g fiber, 1,017 mg sodium

Cocido

Cocido is a traditional dish in parts of South America and the Caribbean. It's a robust mix of poultry, meats, vegetables, spices, and herbs. It usually contains some potatoes. If the rest of your family wants them, you can leave them in and just pluck them out of your serving. Cocido includes so many other kinds of delicious ingredients, you won't miss the spuds.

> 2 chicken legs and thighs, most of skin removed
> 3 tablespoons extra-virgin olive oil
> 1 pound beef stew meat, cut into 1-inch cubes
> ½ pound hot chorizo sausages, sliced
> 1 medium onion, coarsely chopped (2 cups)
> 5 cloves garlic, chopped
> ½ small cabbage, cut into wedges
> ½ pound winter squash such as Hubbard, peeled and
>   cubed
> 1 fresh hot chile such as serrano, whole with stem on
> 1 bay leaf
> ½ teaspoon oregano
> 1½ teaspoons apple cider vinegar
> 4 cups beef stock
> Salt and freshly ground black pepper
> 1 ripe plantain or 2 bananas, peeled, cut in half, and
>   sliced lengthwise

1. In a skillet over medium-high heat, cook the chicken in 2 tablespoons oil until lightly browned on both sides, about 10 minutes. Transfer to a large soup kettle or saucepan.

2. In the oil remaining in the skillet, cook the beef and sausages over medium heat, stirring occasionally, 10 minutes. Add to the chicken.

3. In the same skillet, cook the onion until soft and translucent, about 7 minutes, adding most of the

chopped garlic for the last minute of cooking. Transfer to the saucepan, along with the cabbage, squash, chile, bay leaf, oregano, vinegar, and beef stock.

4. Cover and simmer until all the ingredients, including the beef, are tender, about 1 hour or longer. Season with salt and pepper.

5. While the stew is simmering, heat the remaining 1 tablespoon oil in a skillet, and add the plantains and remaining garlic. Cook until the plantains are golden on all sides, about 10 minutes. Add to the stew for the last minutes of cooking. By now, the cooking liquids and softened vegetables will have become a thick broth.

6. Remove the hot pepper and bay leaf. Serve the cocido in large individual soup bowls with a soup spoon and fork, and dig in!

Serves 6

Nutrition information: Per serving: 494 calories, 43% fat (23.9 g; 6.6 g saturated), 18% carbs (23.1 g), 39% protein (46.7 g), 145 mg cholesterol, 3.3 g fiber, 903 mg sodium

Seafood Dishes

Seafood is carb-free, high in protein, and low in saturated fat. It's best prepared in ways that bring out its distinct, subtle flavors. You can sauté, broil, grill, bake, or poach it—just don't overcook it. Enhance it with flavored butters, oil, sauces, salsas, and vinaigrettes—the possibilities are endless.

- **Sole meunière:** In this simple French preparation of sole, fillets of fish are dredged in flour, sautéed in butter and olive oil, and served with lemon slices and fresh parsley. You can substitute any mild fish fillet.
- **Fish tacos:** After marinating and grilling swordfish, halibut, or any other firm fish, you can slice it and serve it with shredded lettuce and your favorite salsa wrapped in a low-carb tortilla.
- **Seafood gumbo:** This thick stew originated in Louisiana and is traditionally made with shrimp, scallops, lobster, and crab combined with sausage and bell peppers, onions, tomatoes, and most importantly, okra.

Shrimp with Garlic, Chile, and Herbs

This scrumptious shrimp dish needs no sales pitch with all its lively seasonings. Low-glycemic-load eating is a pleasure with dishes like this one. You can use fresh or frozen shrimp sold in most supermarkets.

1 medium tomato, chopped
1 hot chile such as serrano, chopped
2 tablespoons extra-virgin olive oil, divided
½ cup fresh cilantro leaves
2 tablespoons mint leaves
1 pound shrimp, peeled and deveined, with tails left on
4 cloves garlic, minced
½ teaspoon salt

1. In a large skillet, cook the tomato and chile in 1 tablespoon oil over medium heat until somewhat softened, about 5 minutes.

2. Put the cilantro and mint in a food processor fitted with a metal blade, and add the tomato and chile. Process to the consistency of a sauce.

3. Heat the remaining 1 tablespoon oil in the skillet over medium heat. Add the shrimp. Sauté, stirring occasionally, 2 minutes. Add the garlic and salt; stir and cook 2 more minutes until the shrimp are nearly opaque.

4. Reduce heat to low, and pour in the tomato mixture. Stir to combine ingredients. Cook until the shrimp are opaque but still tender, about 5 minutes. Serve immediately. Tasty accompaniments are black beans cooked with a clove of garlic; vinaigrette salad made with avocado, tomato, and sweet pepper; and Mexican beer.

Serves 4

Nutrition information: Per serving: 191 calories, 38% fat (8.2 g; 1.3 g saturated), 8% carbs (4.0 g), 53% protein (24.6 g), 221 mg cholesterol, 1.3 g fiber, 738 mg sodium

Salmon with Mushrooms and Crème Fraîche

Salmon steaks and fillets can be dry, but there's little chance of that with this recipe. The fish is gently cooked on low heat and served with a creamy sauce that moistens every last mouthful of this delectable dish. And wait until you taste the combination of salmon and fragrant mushrooms, a surprisingly compatible pairing of flavors. Add some green peas or a salad, and you have yourself an elegant meal fit for company.

> 3 tablespoons unrefined safflower oil
> 3 cloves garlic, minced
> 8 ounces mixed fresh mushrooms such as cremini, oyster, shiitake, and porcini
> 4 (4-ounce) salmon fillets or steaks, about ¾ inch thick
> Salt
> ½ cup crème fraîche (see Note)
> 1 teaspoon lemon juice
> 1 tablespoon minced fresh parsley

1. In a large skillet over medium heat, warm the oil. Add the garlic, and cook 1 minute, taking care that the garlic does not brown. Add the mushrooms, and sauté, stirring frequently, 2 minutes.

2. Lay the salmon fillets, skin side down, or salmon steaks on the bed of mushrooms in the skillet. Season the fish and vegetables with salt. Cover the skillet, lower the heat, and cook until the flesh of the fish is no longer opaque but is still moist, about 6 minutes. Using a slotted spatula, transfer the fish and mushrooms to dinner plates.

3. Add the crème fraîche to the liquid remaining in the skillet. If the sauce is scant or too thick, add 1 or 2 tablespoons water. Stir in the lemon juice, and season to taste. Add the parsley, stir, and spoon the sauce over the fish.

Note: A French specialty, crème fraîche has a slightly tangy, nutty flavor and velvety rich texture. It can be boiled without curdling, making it an ideal addition to sauces such as this one.

Serves 4

Nutrition information: Per serving: 342 calories, 56% fat (21.4 g; 5.2 g saturated), 7% carbs (5.9 g), 38% protein (31.4 g), 89 mg cholesterol, 0.8 g fiber, 358 mg sodium

Shrimp with Feta and Tomatoes

A friend served my wife and me this dish one summer night on the deck overlooking the garden that produced some of the fresh ingredients. We are glad she was willing to share the recipe because we have enjoyed it many times since then. Because it has the consistency of a stew, serve it in a shallow soup bowl, and provide a spoon to ensure none of the delicious sauce goes uneaten.

> **2 large onions, thinly sliced**
> **⅓ cup olive oil**
> **2 cloves garlic, minced**
> **4 large tomatoes, peeled and coarsely chopped**
> **2 teaspoons fresh dill or oregano, your choice**
> **3 tablespoons chopped fresh parsley**
> **¼ teaspoon sugar**
> **⅛ teaspoon pepper**
> **2 pounds raw peeled shrimp**
> **1 pound feta cheese**

1. Preheat oven to 450°F.

2. Sauté onions in the oil in an ovenproof skillet until yellow and tender. Add garlic, and sauté briefly.

3. Add the tomatoes, dill or oregano, parsley, sugar, and pepper. Cover and simmer 30 minutes, stirring occasionally.

4. Add the shrimp, and mix with the sauce. Crumble the feta on top, and bring to a boil.

5. Bake uncovered 15 minutes. Ladle into bowls, and serve.

Serves 4

Nutrition information: Per serving: 1,068 calories, 58% fat (69.2 g; 37.1 g saturated), 11% carbs (29.0 g), 32% protein (82.2 g), 644 mg cholesterol, 4.2 g fiber, 1,243 mg sodium

Weeknight Fish Stew

This concoction of seafood and vegetables tastes like a compli-
cated dish but goes together quickly—especially if you buy fish
with all bones removed and deveined shrimp. Of course, you can
make the stew more elaborate by adding shellfish and sausage, but
this version delivers lots of flavor as it is. Parsnips add sweetness.

> 2 tablespoons extra-virgin olive oil
> 1 cup chopped onion
> 2 parsnips, peeled and cut into 1-inch chunks
> 2 carrots, peeled and cut into 1-inch chunks
> 1 (15-ounce) can no-salt-added chicken broth
> 1 (15-ounce) can stewed tomatoes
> Tabasco or other hot sauce, to taste
> 2 cloves garlic, minced
> 1¼ pounds assorted fish, such as cod, halibut, and red
>   snapper, skin and bones removed
> 12 large deveined shrimp, shells removed
> ¼ pound spinach, thoroughly washed and coarsely
>   chopped
> Salt and freshly ground pepper, to taste

1. Heat the oil over medium-high heat in a large saucepan
   with a lid. Add the onion, and cook, stirring frequently.
   Sauté until the onion softens and becomes translucent,
   about 7 minutes.

2. Add the parsnips, carrots, chicken broth, and tomatoes.
   Cover and cook on medium-high heat until the
   vegetables are just tender, about 20 minutes.

3. Stir in the Tabasco and garlic. Add the fish, submerging
   it in the tomato sauce as much as possible. Cook on
   medium heat until the fish is opaque and tender but not
   falling apart, 5 to 10 minutes.

4. Add the shrimp, and cook 2 minutes. Immediately add the spinach, cover the pot, and cook the spinach until it wilts, 2 to 3 minutes. At this point, the shrimp should be pink all over but still tender. Season with salt and pepper. Serve with a green salad.

Serves 4

Nutrition information: Per serving: 429 calories, 21% fat (9.9 g; 1.6 g saturated), 32% carbs (34.8 g), 47% protein (49.3 g), 154 mg cholesterol, 8.5 g fiber, 541 mg sodium

Grilled Halibut with Lemon-Herb Splash

(From Dishing by Kathy Casey)

If grilling is not your thing, you can pan-sear or bake the fish. Sea bass is a delicious alternative to the halibut. The lemon-herb splash also makes a great marinade for grilled prawns or sea scallops.

> 6 tablespoons extra-virgin olive oil
> 2 tablespoons fresh lemon juice
> 2 teaspoons lemon zest
> 1½ teaspoons minced fresh rosemary
> 1½ teaspoons minced fresh basil
> 1 tablespoon minced fresh parsley
> ⅛ teaspoon dried red pepper flakes
> ½ teaspoon minced garlic
> ¼ teaspoon salt
> 4 (6-ounce) halibut steaks or fillets
> Oil as needed
> Salt and black pepper

1. To make the lemon-herb splash, mix together the olive oil, lemon juice, lemon zest, rosemary, basil, parsley, red pepper flakes, garlic, and salt. Refrigerate until needed.

2. Preheat the grill. Lightly rub the fish on each side with a little oil, and season with salt and pepper as desired.

3. Grill the fish 2 to 3 minutes per side, depending on the thickness of the fish. The fish should be nicely grill-marked and cooked through but still juicy.

4. Place the fish on plates, and splash each piece of fish with 1 tablespoon or more of the lemon-herb splash. Pass the remaining splash on the side.

Chef's tip: To add a light smoky flavor, soak a few wood chips, such as apple, mesquite, or pecan (depending upon where you live), in water. Throw them on the coals just before placing the fish on the grill.

Serves 4

Nutrition information: Per serving: 420 calories, 54% fat (25.2 g; 3.4 g saturated), 1% carbs (0.8 g), 45% protein (45.5 g), 70 mg cholesterol, 0.1 g fiber, 357 mg sodium

Vegetable Side Dishes

Perhaps you wonder if your plate will look empty after you've eliminated bread, potatoes, and rice. Don't worry; there are so many delicious ways to serve vegetable dishes, you won't miss the starchy staples. If you move beyond simply steaming vegetables or cooking them in the microwave, you'll find they can be anything but boring. Try some of the great sides in this list and the following recipes:

- **Feta green beans:** Steam green beans until still slightly crunchy. Serve at room temperature, and sprinkle with feta cheese, fresh mint, and pine nuts.
- **Parmesan asparagus:** Roast asparagus in the oven at high heat in balsamic vinegar and olive oil until crispy, and then sprinkle with Parmesan cheese.
- **Broccoli and almonds:** Sauté broccoli with butter, lemon juice, and toasted almond slices.
- **Cauliflower au gratin:** Steam cauliflower (or another vegetable), combine it with a white sauce, top it with cheese, and bake until golden brown.
- **Mushroom medley:** Sauté a variety of mushrooms in butter.
- **Fresh artichokes:** Steam artichokes, and serve them with melted butter or your favorite dipping sauce.
- **Portobello mushrooms:** Roast or grill the mushrooms, and sprinkle them with fresh herbs and goat cheese.
- **Scalloped summer squash:** Cube and steam squash and then bake with sautéed onions, garlic, and bell pepper topped with Parmesan cheese.
- **Ricotta tomatoes:** Stuff tomato halves with spinach and ricotta cheese, and bake until filling begins to bubble.

Southern Leafy Greens and Bacon

Dark leafy greens like kale have a slightly bitter, earthy flavor that can hold its own with robust meat entrées such as roast pork or beef stew. The crispy bacon, onion, garlic, currants, and apple cider vinegar add savory, sweet, and tart notes, turning greens into a highly entertaining dish. For a variation, mix the kale with other dark leafy greens such as collard, turnip, and mustard greens.

> ½ teaspoon salt
> 1½ pounds kale, stems removed, thoroughly washed
>   and coarsely chopped
> 2 slices bacon, cut crosswise into strips
> 1 tablespoon extra-virgin olive oil
> 1 medium onion, chopped fine
> 1 clove garlic, minced
> 2 tablespoons currants
> Apple cider vinegar, about 2 teaspoons

1. Fill a large pot with water, and bring to a boil. Put the salt and then the kale into the pot, and cook 2 minutes, stirring, until the greens wilt. Cover the pot, and cook until the kale is tender, about 7 minutes.

2. Meanwhile, fry the bacon in a large skillet over medium heat, until crisp, about 5 minutes. Cover a plate with paper towels, and place the bacon on this to drain fat.

3. When the kale is tender, pour it into a colander. Rinse the pot with cold water, so that it quickly cools, and refill with cold water. Return the kale to the pot to stop the greens from cooking further. Lift the kale out of the pot in handfuls, squeezing it until almost dry, and then collect the kale in a bowl. Set aside.

4. Discard the bacon fat in the skillet, and add the oil. Add the onion, and sauté over medium heat until soft, about 3 minutes. Add the garlic, and cook 30 seconds.

5. Add the kale, bacon, and currants. Cover the skillet, and reheat the greens, cooking about 2 minutes. If liquid accumulates, cook the kale mixture uncovered an additional minute. Sprinkle with apple cider vinegar, stir once, and serve immediately.

Serves 4

Nutrition information: Per serving: 114 calories, 40% fat (5.5 g; 1.1 g saturated), 47% carbs (14.7 g), 13% protein (4.0 g), 3 mg cholesterol, 3.5 g fiber, 556 mg sodium

Asian Asparagus Vinaigrette

To spark the flavor of hot vegetables, treat them to a vinegar and oil dressing. This simple recipe takes well to variation. You can use broccoli or green beans instead of asparagus. You can also add some garlic, a dash of sesame oil, or a tablespoon of bottled hoisin sauce—a sweet and spicy condiment used in Chinese cooking and available in many supermarkets.

> **1 pound asparagus, tough ends snapped off**
> **1 tablespoon minced fresh gingerroot**
> **2 tablespoons seasoned rice wine vinegar**
> **1 tablespoon soy sauce**
> **1 tablespoon unrefined safflower oil**

1. Fit a large pot with a steamer basket, and fill it with enough water to nearly reach the bottom of the basket. Bring the water to a boil. Add the asparagus, and cover with a tight-fitting lid. Cook over medium-high heat until the stalks compress slightly when squeezed and the asparagus bends slightly when picked up, about 5 minutes.

2. Meanwhile, in a small bowl, whisk together the gingerroot, vinegar, soy sauce, and oil.

3. When the asparagus is done, transfer it to a platter, and drizzle with the dressing. Serve with steamed fish, steak, and Asian dishes.

Serves 4

Nutrition information: Per serving: 72 calories, 41% fat (3.6 g; 0.4 g saturated), 45% carbs (9.3 g), 14% protein (2.7 g), 0 mg cholesterol, 2.4 g fiber, 259 mg sodium

Braised Leeks

Leeks—the uptown version of onions—have a subtle, sweet flavor that makes them an elegant side dish and a lovely complement to soups and stews. Yet they are not a staple in American kitchens, in part because they are pricier than ordinary onions and because prepping these large, seemingly ungainly stalks is unfamiliar territory. So here's a chance to get to know leeks and enjoy them forevermore. This unadorned recipe features the delicate flavor of these special onions.

> **4 thick leeks or 6 medium leeks**
> **3 tablespoons extra-virgin olive oil**
> **Vegetable stock or water**
> **2 sprigs parsley**
> **Salt and freshly ground pepper**
> **1 tablespoon freshly squeezed lemon juice**

1. To trim the leeks, remove any leaves that are withered or yellowed. Cut off the root end and the tough upper portion of the green tops, leaving only a few inches of darker green above the pale green stalk.

2. Leeks often contain a lot of sand. To wash, cut the length of each leek, beginning about one inch from the root end and making a slit down the center of each stalk. With your fingertips, fan out the leaves somewhat, and rinse in a bowl or under cold running water. When the leeks are thoroughly cleaned, cut them into 4-inch lengths.

3. Put the leeks in a sauté pan or shallow casserole, arranging them so they lie flat and straight. Add the oil and ½ cup stock or water—enough to cover the leeks. Add the parsley, and season with salt and pepper. Cover the pan, and cook, turning occasionally, until the leeks are very tender and can be easily pierced with a fork, 15

to 25 minutes, depending on the freshness and thickness of the leeks.

4. When the leeks are tender, uncover the pan, raise the heat, and boil away all the liquid. In the process, the leeks will begin to lightly brown. Sprinkle with the lemon juice, and serve hot, at room temperature, or cold.

Serves 4

Nutrition information: Per serving: 126 calories, 70% fat (10.3 g; 1.4 g saturated), 27% carbs (9.0 g), 3% protein (1.0 g), 0 mg cholesterol, 1.2 g fiber, 280 mg sodium

Cheese-Stuffed Peppers Two Ways

This colorful dish is a great accompaniment to grilled foods and is especially good when fresh peppers and tomatoes are in season.

3 bell peppers, preferably yellow or orange

Stuffing option 1
1½ teaspoons olive oil
1½ tablespoons balsamic vinegar
1 clove garlic, minced
¾ pound tomatoes of choice, seeded and coarsely
    chopped
1 cup fresh mozzarella cheese cubes
½ cup fresh basil leaves cut into strips
Salt and pepper to taste

Stuffing option 2
1 tablespoon olive oil
¾ pound tomatoes of choice, seeded and coarsely
    chopped
1 cup feta cheese cubes
½ cup quartered, pitted kalamata olives
Fresh or dried oregano
Salt and pepper to taste

1. Preheat oven to 375°F.

2. Cut the peppers in half lengthwise, and remove seeds and ribs. Set aside.

3. Combine all the ingredients for either filling in a bowl, and stuff each pepper with the filling.

4. Place in a greased baking dish, and bake until the peppers are tender, about 40 minutes.

Serves 4

Nutrition information (with mozzarella): Per serving: 128 calories, 54% fat (8.1 g; 3.9 g saturated), 25% carbs (8.7 g), 20% protein (6.7 g), 22 mg cholesterol, 2.0 g fiber, 113 mg sodium

Nutrition information (with feta): Per serving: 160 calories, 71% fat (13 g; 6.2 g saturated), 14% carbs (6.0 g), 15% protein (5.9 g), 33 mg cholesterol, 1.6 g fiber, 548 mg sodium

Cumin-Grilled Zucchini with Tomato-Corn Salsa

(From Dishing *by Kathy Casey)*

"These vegetables can be served hot or at room temperature. It's a great dish to take to a summer barbecue or picnic potluck."
—Kathy Casey

Tomato-Corn Salsa
¾ cup diced ripe tomatoes (¼ inch dice)
1 cup (about 1 ear) fresh, sweet corn kernels
¼ cup finely diced red onion
1 fresh jalapeño, seeded and minced
1 tablespoon red wine vinegar
2 tablespoons olive oil
2 tablespoons chopped fresh cilantro
¾ teaspoon salt
¼ teaspoon cumin

Zucchini
1 tablespoon olive oil
1 teaspoon cumin
½ teaspoon salt
¼ teaspoon black pepper
3 medium (about 1¼ pounds) zucchini
Sour cream

1. To make the salsa, in a large bowl, mix all of the ingredients together well. Some jalapeños are hotter than others, so try a little piece before mixing it all in, and then adjust the amount of jalapeño as needed for the desired spiciness.

2. Get the coals going for a very hot grill.

3. In a large bowl, mix together the olive oil, cumin, salt, and pepper. Cut the zucchini in half lengthwise, and add them to the bowl. Rub the oil mixture over the zucchini, making sure they are coated well.

4. Place the zucchini over very hot coals, and grill 2 to 3 minutes on each side to mark the zucchini nicely. Cook until just done. Depending on how hot the grill is and how done you like your vegetables, the total cooking time can vary from 4 to 10 minutes.

5. Serve the zucchini topped with the salsa and a dollop or squiggle of sour cream.

Serves 4

Nutrition information: Per serving: 185 calories, 63% fat (13.9 g; 3.4 g saturated), 29% carbs (14.9 g), 8% protein (3.8 g), 6 mg cholesterol, 3.4 g fiber, 1,214 mg sodium

Desserts and Sweets

You can satisfy your sweet tooth and still keep your glycemic load down. The trick is to use desserts and sweets to stimulate your taste buds, not to fill up on. This is where the difference between glycemic index and glycemic load becomes crucial. You can enjoy foods with high glycemic *indexes*, as long as you don't eat enough to raise your glycemic *load*. If the sugar isn't diluted with starch, as it is in cookies, cakes, and pastries, a typical-size serving after a meal shouldn't cause a glucose shock. Be careful, though; sweets are so pleasing to the palate that you might get carried away, even when you're not hungry. So enjoy these dessert options in moderation.

- **Chocolate:** From the finest dark chocolate truffle to the ubiquitous chocolate chip, chocolate is your friend as long as you use it to satisfy your sweet tooth, not your hunger. The glycemic load of dark or semisweet chocolate is lower than that of milk chocolate. I keep Ghirardelli double-chocolate, dark chocolate chips in the freezer and grab some when I have a craving for something sweet. Just remember the rules: eat them after a meal, and don't eat more than you can wrap the fingers of one hand around.
- **Chocolate-covered nuts:** Nuts are carb-free, and there isn't enough sugar in a coating of chocolate to make much of an impact, as long as this candy is consumed in moderation. (See the recipe for Daisy's Chocolate-Covered Almonds.)
- **Peanut brittle, peppermint candy, and jelly beans:** These nonstarchy candies are fine as long as you consume them only after a meal and don't eat more than you can wrap your fingers around.
- **Sugar-free ice cream:** The high sugar content of most ice creams results in unacceptable glycemic loads. However,

some companies are making no-sugar-added ice creams, which have low glycemic loads. Be careful not to confuse these with low-*fat* ice creams, which are usually very high in sugar.

Lemon-Scented Macaroons

The richness of coconut marries well with the tartness of citrus in these macaroons. They go together and bake in a jiffy to give you the ideal garnish for a mixed-fruit dessert of sliced fresh oranges and banana.

> **2 egg whites**
> **1 teaspoon vanilla**
> **Zest of 1 lemon, preferably organic**
> **2½ cups coconut**
> **¾ cup sugar**
> **Pinch of salt**

1. Preheat the oven to 350°F. Cover a baking sheet with parchment paper.

2. Briefly beat the egg whites, vanilla, and lemon zest in a large bowl with a fork. Add the coconut, sugar, and salt. Combine the ingredients, using a wooden spoon or your hands.

3. Manually make small piles of the mixture, each about 1 heaping teaspoon, and set them on the baking sheet about 1 inch apart. Bake until lightly browned, about 15 minutes.

4. Remove the baking sheet from the oven, and place it on a metal rack, allowing the cookies to cool 30 minutes. Transfer the cookies to a decorative plate, and serve with fruit compote.

Note: The macaroons will keep in a sealed container for several days—if they last that long!

Makes 24 cookies, 2 per serving

Nutrition information: Per serving: 74 calories, 40% fat (3.4 g; 3.0 g saturated), 57% carbs (10.9 g), 3% protein (0.6 g), 0 mg cholesterol, 0.4 g fiber, 49 mg sodium

Daisy's Chocolate-Covered Almonds

When a longtime patient of mine, Daisy Wing, heard I like chocolate and nuts, she made me a batch of these delicious chocolate almond clusters. I enjoyed them so much that I talked her into divulging her technique. They make a wonderful low-glycemic-load dessert.

1 pound raw almonds
½ pound semisweet chocolate

1. Preheat the oven to 275°F. Spread the almonds evenly on a baking pan.

2. Roast the almonds 1 hour and 40 minutes. Stir them every 15 minutes, so they roast evenly. Remove them from the oven, and let them cool.

3. Put the chocolate in a glass bowl, and microwave it for 2 minutes on medium until melted.

4. While the almonds are still warm, mix them into the melted chocolate. Use a spoon to scoop out clusters of approximately 10 chocolate-covered almonds each. Use a spatula to scrape the clusters off the spoon onto a tray lined with waxed paper.

5. Allow the candy to cool until the chocolate is hard.

Note: Store in an airtight container in the freezer for up to 6 months.

Makes approximately 4 dozen clusters

Nutrition information: Per cluster: 164 calories, 71% fat (5.4 g; 0 g saturated), 19% carbs (3.2 g), 10% protein (1.8 g), 0 mg cholesterol, 1.4 g fiber, 44 mg sodium

Raspberry-Studded Mini Cheesecakes with Pignoli Crust

Top off a low-glycemic-load meal with one of these and you're sure to feel well fed and satisfied. Instead of the standard graham cracker crust made with flour, these cheesecakes have a base of rich, fragrant pine nuts, called pignolis in Italian. While making mini cheesecakes takes more effort than baking just one big cake, it guarantees portion control—that is, if you don't eat a half dozen at once!

>24 1½-inch-diameter paper cup liners
>½ cup pignolis
>2 eggs, separated
>12 ounces cream cheese
>5 tablespoons sugar, divided
>½ lemon, zest and juice
>1½ teaspoons all-purpose flour
>1½ cups sour cream
>1 teaspoon vanilla
>24 raspberries

1. Place the paper liners in the cups of a 24-cup muffin tin. Preheat the oven to 325°F.

2. Put pignolis in a food processor fitted with a metal blade, and process until the nuts have the coarse texture of bread crumbs, 3 to 4 seconds. Sprinkle the nuts into the muffin cups, and manually press down to form a bottom crust for the cheesecake.

3. In a medium-size bowl, using an electric mixer, beat the egg yolks until light. Add the cream cheese, 4 tablespoons sugar, and the lemon zest and juice. Beat until smooth. Stir in the flour.

4. Beat the egg whites until they hold soft peaks. Using a rubber spatula, fold the whites into the cheese mixture. Spoon the batter into the prepared muffin tin. Place the tin in a water bath (see Note). Carefully transfer to the oven. Bake until the cake is very lightly browned and just set, about 50 minutes. Remove the cheesecake, and turn up the oven to 450°F.

5. In a small bowl, combine the sour cream, the remaining 1 tablespoon sugar, and the vanilla. Spread over the top of each cheesecake. Return the muffin tin filled with cheesecakes to the oven, without the baking pan, and bake 5 minutes. Remove the tin, and set on a rack to cool. Cover loosely with plastic wrap, and refrigerate until well chilled.

6. To serve, insert a fresh raspberry into the center of each cheesecake. Alternatively, if using frozen berries, insert the berries in the warm cheesecakes before they cool, to defrost the fruit, and then refrigerate. (If the cheesecakes are to be eaten over several days, add the fruit just before serving.)

Note: A water bath promotes more even cooking. Use a baking pan larger than the muffin tin, and place the tin in the pan. Add warm water to the baking pan until it comes at least halfway up the height of the muffin tin.

Makes 12 servings of 1 cake

Nutrition information: Per serving: 60 calories, 74% fat (5 g; 2.7 g saturated), 16% carbs (2.5 g), 10% protein (1.5 g), 20 mg cholesterol, 0.2 g fiber, 30 mg sodium

Warm Caramelized Pears with Roasted Pecans and Ice Cream

These pears are cooked in a butterscotch sauce that, as it cooks down, eventually caramelizes the pears. Add richly fragrant pecans, top the warm pears with a small amount of cool ice cream, and you have an intensely pleasurable dessert. This dish is easy to make. The only challenge is keeping to a modest portion. Remember, ¾ cup of ice cream is meant to serve six.

> 2 Bosc pears
> 1 cup water
> 2 tablespoons butterscotch topping
> Zest of ½ lemon (1 tablespoon)
> 1 teaspoon butter
> ¼ cup pecans
> ¾ cup premium vanilla ice cream

1. Cut the pears in half lengthwise, and remove their cores. Cut each half lengthwise into narrow slices. Put the water and butterscotch in a medium-size saucepan, and stir to combine. Add the pears and lemon zest.

2. Cook the pears over medium heat, stirring occasionally. After about 30 minutes, the pears will have reduced in size, and most of the cooking liquid will have evaporated. Continue cooking until the remaining caramel sauce is very thick and begins to coat the fruit, an additional 10 minutes.

3. Meanwhile, put the butter in a small skillet; add the pecans, and toast over medium heat, stirring frequently, until the nuts become fragrant, about 5 minutes. Remove from heat, and set aside.

4. To assemble the dessert, place 3 or 4 pear slices on a salad plate or in a stemmed glass. Using a spoon slightly larger than a standard flatware teaspoon, scoop a spoonful of ice cream, and top the warm pear with the ice cream, plus a few pecans. Proceed with the other servings, or refrigerate the remaining pear and pecans for later use.

Serves 6

Nutrition information: Per serving: 130 calories, 44% fat (6.6 g; 2.3 g saturated), 52% carbs (18.1 g), 5% protein (1.5 g), 9 mg cholesterol, 2.0 g fiber, 36 mg sodium

Concluding Remarks

IF YOU ARE overweight, it's not simply because you lack will-power. Chances are you have a genetic proclivity to insulin resistance. However, that tendency wouldn't be a problem if your diet didn't cause excessive glucose shocks and your slow-twitch muscle fibers didn't spend too much time in the sleep mode. To relieve insulin resistance, you need to reduce the glycemic load of your diet and restore your muscles' sensitivity to insulin. Part 2 of this book showed you how, with little deprivation or inconvenience, you can eliminate the glucose shocks that drive up your insulin levels and encourage your body to store calories as fat. It also showed you how you can, without strenuous exertion, switch on your muscles' sensitivity to insulin and counteract the metabolic shutdown that interferes with weight loss.

When, instead of trying to starve yourself, you correct the disturbances that caused you to gain weight in the first place, you'll probably experience a sense of optimism—and for good reason. You will not only feel better physically but will have made an important discovery about your health and your ability to change it, a discovery that will allow you to enjoy life more as your weight returns to normal. I know what people can and cannot do when it comes to making changes in their lives. This is something you *can* do.

Appendix A

Glycemic Loads of Common Foods

Food Item	Description	Available Carbohydrate (%)	Typical Serving	Glycemic Load
Lab standard:				
white bread	30 g	47	N/A	100
Baked Goods				
Oatmeal cookie	1 medium	68	1 oz.	102
Apple muffin, sugarless	2½-in. diameter	32	2½ oz.	107
Cookie: average, all types	1 medium	64	1 oz.	114
Croissant	1 medium	46	1½ oz.	127
Crumpet	1 medium	38	2 oz.	148
Bran muffin	2½-in. diameter	42	2 oz.	149
Pastry	Average serving	46	2 oz.	149
Chocolate cake	1 slice (4″ x 4″ x 1″)	47	3 oz.	154
Vanilla wafers	4 wafers	72	1 oz.	159
Graham cracker	1 rectangle	72	1 oz.	159
Blueberry muffin	2½-in. diameter	51	2 oz.	169
Pita	1 medium	57	2 oz.	189
Carrot cake	1 square (3″ x 3″ x 1½″)	56	2 oz.	199
Carrot muffin	2½-in. diameter	56	2 oz.	199

Food Item	Description	Available Carbohydrate (%)	Typical Serving	Glycemic Load
Baked Goods (continued)				
Waffle	7-in. diameter	37	2½ oz.	203
Doughnut	1 medium	49	2 oz.	205
Cupcake	2½-in. diameter	68	1½ oz.	213
Angel food cake	1 slice (4" x 4" x 1")	58	2 oz.	216
English muffin	1 medium	47	2 oz.	224
Pound cake	1 slice (4" x 4" x 1")	53	3 oz.	241
Corn muffin	2½-in. diameter	51	2 oz.	299
Pancake	5-in. diameter	73	2½ oz.	346
Alcoholic Beverages				
Spirits	1½ oz.	0	1½ oz.	<15
Red wine	6-oz. glass	0	6 oz.	<15
White wine	6-oz. glass	0	6 oz.	<15
Beer	12-oz. can/bottle	3	12 oz.	<15
Nonalcoholic Beverages				
Tomato juice	8-oz. glass	4	8 oz.	36
Chocolate milk	8-oz. glass	10	8 oz.	82
Carrot juice	8-oz. glass	12	8 oz.	91
Grapefruit juice, unsweetened	8-oz. glass	9	8 oz.	100
Apple juice, unsweetened	8-oz. glass	12	8 oz.	109
Orange juice	8-oz. glass	10	8 oz.	119
Raspberry smoothie	8-oz. glass	16	8 oz.	127
Cranberry juice	8-oz. glass	12	8 oz.	145
Pineapple juice, unsweetened	8-oz. glass	14	8 oz.	145
Coca-Cola	12-oz. can	10	12 oz.	218
Gatorade	20-oz. bottle	6	20 oz.	273
Orange soda	12-oz. can	14	12 oz.	314

Breads and Rolls

Tortilla, wheat	1 medium	52	1¾ oz.	80
Pizza crust	1 slice	22	3½ oz.	70
White bread	1 slice, ½ in. thick	47	1 oz.	107
Wholemeal rye bread	⅜-in. slice	40	2 oz.	114
Sourdough bread	⅜-in. slice	47	1½ oz.	114
Tortilla, corn	1 medium	48	1¾ oz.	120
Oat bran bread	⅜-in. slice	60	1½ oz.	128
Whole wheat bread	1 slice, ½ in. thick	43	1½ oz.	129
Light rye bread	⅜-in. slice	47	1½ oz.	142
Banana bread, sugarless	1 slice (4″ x 4″ x 1″)	48	3 oz.	170
80% whole-kernel oat bread	⅜-in. slice	63	1½ oz.	170
Pita	8-in. diameter	57	2 oz.	189
Hamburger bun	Top and bottom, 5-in. diameter	50	2½ oz.	213
80% whole-kernel wheat bread	⅜-in. slice	67	2¼ oz.	213
French bread	1 slice, ½ in. thick	50	2 oz.	284
Bagel	1 medium	50	3⅓ oz.	340

Breakfast Cereals

All-Bran	½ cup	77	1 oz.	85
Muesli	1 cup	53	1 oz.	95
Special K	1 cup	70	1 oz.	133
Cheerios	1 cup	40	1 oz.	142
Shredded wheat	1 cup	67	1 oz.	142
Grape-Nuts	1 cup	70	1 oz.	142
Puffed wheat	1 cup	70	1 oz.	151
Instant oatmeal (cooked)	1 cup	10	8 oz.	154
Cream of Wheat (cooked)	1 cup	10	8 oz.	154
Total	1 cup	73	1 oz.	161

Food Item	Description	Available Carbohydrate (%)	Typical Serving	Glycemic Load
Breakfast Cereals (continued)				
Cornflakes	1 cup	77	1 oz.	199
Rice Krispies	1 cup	87	1 oz.	208
Rice Chex	1 cup	87	1 oz.	218
Raisin bran	1 cup	63	2 oz.	227
Candy				
Life Saver	1 piece	100	1/10 oz.	20
Peanut M&M's	1 snack-size package	57	3/4 oz.	43
White chocolate	2 squares (1" x 1" x 1/4")	44	2/3 oz.	49
Chocolate	2 squares (1" x 1" x 1/4")	44	1 oz.	68
Snickers bar	1 regular-size bar	57	2 oz.	218
Jelly beans	1/3 cup	93	1 1/2 oz.	312
Chips and Crackers				
Potato chips	1 small bag	42	1 oz.	62
Corn chips	1 package	52	1 oz.	97
Popcorn	4 cups	55	1 oz.	114
Rye crisps	1 rectangle	64	1 oz.	125
Wheat Thins	4 small	68	1 oz.	136
Soda cracker	2 regular-size	68	1 oz.	136
Pretzels	Small bag	67	1 oz.	151
Dairy Products				
Eggs	2 regular size	0	1 1/2 oz.	<15
Cheese	1 slice (2" x 2" x 1")	0	2 oz.	<15
Butter	1 tablespoon	0	1/4 oz.	<15
Margarine	1 tablespoon	0	1/4 oz.	<15
Sour cream	2 tablespoons	0	1/2 oz.	<15
Yogurt, plain unsweetened	1/2 cup	5	4 oz.	17

Milk, whole	8-oz. glass	5	8 oz.	27
Yogurt, low-fat sweetened	½ cup	16	4 oz.	57
Vanilla ice cream, high-fat	½ cup	18	4 oz.	68
Milk, low-fat chocolate	8-oz. glass	10	8 oz.	82
Vanilla ice cream, low-fat	½ cup	20	4 oz.	114
Frozen tofu dessert	½ cup	30	4 oz.	379

Fruit

Strawberries	1 cup	3	5½ oz.	13
Apricot	1 medium	8	2 oz.	24
Grapefruit	1 half	9	4½ oz.	32
Plum	1 medium	10	3 oz.	36
Kiwifruit	1 medium	10	3 oz.	43
Peach	1 medium	9	4 oz.	47
Grapes	1 cup (40 grapes)	15	2½ oz.	47
Pineapple	1 slice (¾″ thick x 3½″ diam.)	11	3 oz.	50
Watermelon	1 cup cubed	5	5½ oz.	52
Pear	1 medium	9	6 oz.	57
Mango	½ cup	14	3 oz.	57
Orange	1 medium	9	6 oz.	71
Apple	1 medium	13	5½ oz.	78
Banana	1 medium	17	3¼ oz.	85
Raisins	2 tablespoons	73	1 oz.	133
Figs	3 medium	43	2 oz.	151
Dates	5 medium	67	1½ oz.	298

Meat

Beef	10-oz. steak	0	10 oz.	<15
Pork	2 5-oz. chops	0	10 oz.	<15
Chicken	1 breast	0	10 oz.	<15
Fish	8-oz. fillet	0	8 oz.	<15
Lamb	3 4-oz. chops	0	12 oz.	<15

Food Item	Description	Available Carbohydrate (%)	Typical Serving	Glycemic Load
Nuts				
Peanuts	¼ cup	8	1¼ oz.	7
Cashews	¼ cup	26	1¼ oz.	21
Pasta				
Asian bean noodles	1 cup	25	5 oz.	118
Wholemeal spaghetti	1 cup	23	5 oz.	126
Vermicelli	1 cup	24	5 oz.	126
Spaghetti (boiled 5 min.)	1 cup	27	5 oz.	142
Fettucine	1 cup	23	5 oz.	142
Noodles, instant (cooked 2 min.)	1 cup	22	5 oz.	150
Capellini	1 cup	25	5 oz.	158
Spaghetti (boiled 10–15 min.)	1 cup	27	5 oz.	166
Couscous	½ cup	23	4 oz.	174
Linguine	1 cup	25	5 oz.	181
Macaroni	1 cup	28	5 oz.	181
Rice noodles	1 cup	22	5 oz.	181
Spaghetti (boiled 20 min.)	1 cup	24	5 oz.	213
Macaroni and cheese (boxed)	1 cup	28	5 oz.	252
Gnocchi	1 cup	27	5 oz.	260
Soups				
Tomato soup	1 cup	7	8 oz.	55
Minestrone	1 cup	7	8 oz.	64
Lentil soup	1 cup	8	8 oz.	82
Split pea soup	1 cup	11	8 oz.	145
Black bean soup	1 cup	11	8 oz.	154

Sweeteners

Artificial sweeteners	1 teaspoon	0	⅙ oz.	<15
Honey	1 teaspoon	72	⅙ oz.	16
Table sugar	1 round teaspoon	100	⅙ oz.	28
Syrup	¼ cup	100	2 oz.	364

Vegetables

Asparagus	4 spears	6	3 oz.	<15
Broccoli	½ cup	6	1½ oz.	<15
Cucumber	1 cup	2	6 oz.	<15
Lettuce	1 cup	3	2½ oz.	<15
Mushrooms	½ cup	7	2 oz.	<15
Bell pepper	½ medium	4	2 oz.	<15
Spinach	1 cup	5	2½ oz.	<15
Tomato	1 medium	6	5 oz.	<15
Peas	¼ cup	9	1½ oz.	16
Carrot (raw)	1 medium (7½-in. length)	10	3 oz.	21
Carrot (boiled)	½ cup	13	3½ oz.	33
Kidney beans	½ cup	17	3 oz.	40
Navy beans	½ cup	10	3 oz.	40
Garbanzo beans	½ cup	20	3 oz.	45
Lima beans	½ cup	12	3 oz.	57
Pinto beans	½ cup	17	3 oz.	57
Black-eyed peas	½ cup	20	3 oz.	74
Yam	½ cup	24	5 oz.	123
Potato (instant mashed)	¾ cup	13	5 oz.	161
Baked potato	1 medium	20	5 oz.	246
Sweet potato	½ cup	19	5 oz.	161
Corn on the cob	1 ear	21	5⅓ oz.	171
French fries	Medium serving (McDonald's)	19	5¼ oz.	219
Baked potato	1 medium	20	5 oz.	246

Food Item	Description	Available Carbohydrate (%)	Typical Serving	Glycemic Load
Rice				
Rice cakes	1 medium size	84	1 oz.	193
Brown rice	1 cup	22	6½ oz.	222
Basmati rice	1 cup	25	6½ oz.	271
White rice	1 cup	24	6½ oz.	283
Miscellaneous				
Salad dressing	2 tablespoons	6	1 oz.	<15

Appendix B

Converting to Metrics

Volume Measurement Conversions

U.S.	Metric
¼ teaspoon	1.25 ml
½ teaspoon	2.50 ml
¾ teaspoon	3.75 ml
1 teaspoon	5.00 ml
1 tablespoon	15.00 ml
¼ cup	62.50 ml
½ cup	125.00 ml
¾ cup	187.50 ml
1 cup	250.00 ml

Weight Conversion Measurements

U.S.	Metric
1 ounce	28.4 g
8 ounces	227.5 g
16 ounces (1 pound)	455.0 g

Cooking Temperature Conversions

Celsius/Centigrade: 0°C and 100°C are arbitrarily placed at the melting and boiling points of water and standard to the metric system.

Fahrenheit: Fahrenheit established 0°F as the stabilized temperature when equal amounts of ice, water, and salt are mixed.

To convert temperatures in Fahrenheit to Celsius, use this formula:

$$C = (F - 32) \times 0.5555$$

So, for example, if you are baking at 350°F and want to know that temperature in Celsius, use this calculation:

$$C = (350 - 32) \times 0.5555 = 176.65°C$$

Appendix C

References

Aude, Y. W., et al. 2004. The national cholesterol education program diet v. a diet lower in carbohydrates and higher in protein and monounsaturated fat: A randomized trial. *Archives of Internal Medicine* 164:2141–46.

Baer, D. J., et al. 1997. Dietary fiber decreases the metabolizable energy content and nutrient digestibility of mixed diets fed to humans. *Journal of Nutrition* 127 (4): 579–86.

Bond-Brill, J., et al. 2002. Dose-response effect of walking exercise on weight loss: How much is enough? *International Journal of Obesity Related Metabolic Disorders* 26 (11): 1484–93.

Brand-Miller, J. D., et al. 2003. Physiological validation of the concept of glycemic load in lean young adults. *Journal of Nutrition* 133 (9): 2728–32.

Bryner, R. W., et al. 1999. Effects of resistance versus aerobic training combined with an 800 calorie liquid diet on lean body mass and resting metabolic rate. *Journal of the American College of Nutrition* 18 (2): 115–21.

Di Meglio, D. P., and R. D. Mattes. 2000. Liquid versus solid carbohydrate: Effects on food intake and body weight. *International Journal of Obesity Related Metabolic Disorders* 24 (6): 794–800.

Flegal, K. M., et al. 2002. Prevalence and trends in obesity among US adults, 1999–2000. *Journal of the American Medical Association* 288:1728–32.

Fontaine, K. R., et al. 2003. Years of life lost due to obesity. *Journal of the American Medical Association* 289 (2): 187–93.

Foster, G. D., et al. 2003. A randomized trial of a low-carbohydrate diet for obesity. *New England Journal of Medicine* 348 (21): 2082–90.

Foster-Powell, K., S. H. A. Holt, and J. D. Brand-Miller. 2002. International table of glycemic index and glycemic load values. *American Journal of Clinical Nutrition* 76:5–6.

Hays, J. H., et al. 2003. Effects of a high saturated fat and no-starch diet on serum lipid subfractions in patients with documented atherosclerotic cardiovascular disease. *Mayo Clinic Proceedings* 78:1331–36.

Irwin, M. L., et al. 2003. Effect of exercise on total and intra-abdominal body fat in postmenopausal women: A randomized controlled trial. *Journal of the American Medical Association* 289 (3): 323–30.

Jarvi, A. E., et al. 1999. Improved glycemic control and lipid profile and normalized fibrinolytic activity on a low-glycemic index diet in type 2 diabetic patients. *Diabetes Care* 22 (1): 10–18.

Lavin, J. H., et al. 2002. An investigation of the role of oro-sensory stimulation in sugar satiety. *International Journal of Obesity Related Metabolic Disorders* 26 (3): 384–88.

Manson, J. E., et al. 2002. Walking compared with vigorous exercise for the prevention of cardiovascular events in women. *New England Journal of Medicine* 347 (10): 716–25.

Mattes, R. D., and D. Rothacker. 2001. Beverage viscosity is inversely related to postprandial hunger in humans. *Physiological Behavior* 74 (4–5): 551–57.

Miyatake, N., et al. 2002. Daily walking reduces visceral adipose tissue areas and improves insulin resistance in Japanese obese subjects. *Diabetes Research in Clinical Practice* 58 (2): 101–7.

National Center for Health Statistics. 2001. Third National Health and Nutrition Examination Survey. www.cdc.gov/nchs/nhanes.htm (search "body weight").

O'Keefe, J. H., and L. Cordain. 2004. Cardiovascular disease resulting from a diet and lifestyle at odds with our paleolithic genome: How to become a 21st-century hunter-gatherer. *Mayo Clinic Proceedings* 79:101–8.

Packianathan, I. C., et al. 2002. The eating disorder inventory in a UK National Health Service obesity clinic and its response to modest weight loss. *Eating Behavior* 3 (3): 275–84.

Pasman, W. J., et al. 2003. Effect of two breakfasts, different in carbohydrate composition, on hunger and satiety and mood in healthy men. *International Journal of Obesity Related Metabolic Disorders* 27 (6): 663–68.

Pelkman, C. L., et al. 2004. Effects of moderate-fat (from monounsaturated fat) and low-fat weight-loss diets on the serum lipid profile in overweight and obese men and women. *American Journal of Clinical Nutrition* 79:204–12.

Pereira, M. A. 2002. Dairy consumption, obesity, and the insulin resistance syndrome in young adults: The CARDIA study. *Journal of the American Medical Association* 287 (16): 2081–89.

Pereira, M. A., et al. 2004. Effects of a low-glycemic load diet on resting energy expenditure and heart disease risk factors during weight loss. *Journal of the American Medical Association* 292 (20): 2482–90.

Petersen, K. F., et al. 2004. Impaired mitochondrial activity in the insulin-resistant offspring of patients with type 2 diabetes. *New England Journal of Medicine* 350:664–71.

Ryden, A., et al. 2003. Severe obesity and personality: A comparative controlled study of personality traits. *International Journal of Obesity Related Metabolic Disorders* 27 (12): 1534–40.

Samaha, F. F., et al. 2003. A low-carbohydrate as compared with a low-fat diet for severe obesity. *New England Journal of Medicine* 348 (21): 2082–90.

Schulze, M. B. 2004. Sugar-sweetened beverages, weight gain, and incidence of type 2 diabetes in young and middle-aged women. *Journal of the American Medical Association* 292 (8): 927–35.

Slentz, C. A., et al. 2004. Effects of the amount of exercise on body weight, body composition, and measures of central obesity. *Archives of Internal Medicine* 164:31–39.

Sparti, A., et al. 2000. Effects of a diet high or low in unavailable and slowly digested carbohydrates on the pattern of 24 hour substrate oxidation and feelings of hunger in humans. *American Journal of Clinical Nutrition* 72 (6): 1461–68.

Sturm, R. 2003. Increases in clinically severe obesity in the United States 1986–2000. *Archives of Internal Medicine* 163:2146–48.

Taylor, R. 2004. Causation of type 2 diabetes: The Gordian knot unravels. *New England Journal of Medicine* 350:639–41.

Tuomilehto, J., et al. 2004. Coffee consumption and risk of type 2 diabetes mellitus among middle-aged Finnish men and women. *Journal of the American Medical Association* 291 (10): 1213–19.

United States Department of Agriculture, Agricultural Research Service. 2004. National Nutrient Database for Standard Reference, Release 17. Nutrient Data Laboratory Home Page, www.nal.usda.gov/fnic/foodcomp.

Van Wymelbeke, V., et al. 2004. Influence of repeated consumption of beverages containing sucrose or intense sweeteners on food intake. *European Journal of Clinical Nutrition* 58 (1): 154–61.

Warren, J. M., et al. 2003. Low glycemic index breakfasts and reduced food intake in preadolescent children. *Pediatrics* 112 (5): e414.

Watkins, L. L., et al. 2003. Effects of exercise and weight loss on cardiac risk factors associated with Syndrome X. *Archives of Internal Medicine* 163:1889–95.

Westerterp, K. R., and A. D. Kester. 2003. Physical activity in confined conditions as an indicator of free-living physical activity. *Obesity Research* 11 (7): 865–68.

Appendix D

Websites

- **www.lowglycemicload.com** This is a supplement to the book. You will find additional information on such topics as medications, updated glucose-load tables, the latest research, and more recipes. You can also submit questions and comments about your experience with low-glycemic eating.
- **www.americanheart.org/profilers** An interactive tool provided by the American Heart Association for helping people make informed decisions about high blood cholesterol, high blood pressure, and several heart conditions.
- **www.holdthetoast.com** An excellent source for low-glycemic meals and snacks by Dana Carpender, author of *500 Low Carb Recipes: 500 Recipes from Snacks to Desserts the Whole Family Will Love.*
- **www.atkins.com** This website contains hundreds of recipes for low-carbohydrate dishes.
- **www.sugarbusters.com** Delicious low-glycemic-load dishes from New Orleans.

Index

About the Author

Rob Thompson, M.D., is a board-certified cardiologist who has been in private practice in internal medicine and preventive cardiology for more than twenty-eight years. He is also on the active staff at Swedish Medical Center in Seattle, a major regional cardiology referral center. Dr. Thompson is a graduate of the University of Washington School of Medicine, and he completed a residency program in internal medicine and a fellowship in cardiology at the University of Illinois at Chicago. While in academics, Dr. Thompson conducted clinical research and published several articles on cardiovascular topics in peer-reviewed journals, including the *Journal of the American Medical Association, Annals of Internal Medicine,* and *Circulation.* He is the author of *The New Low Carb Way of Life* (M. Evans, 2004), and he has continued to write and publish articles on medical topics in newspapers and magazines, including the *Northwest Physician* and the *Washington State Medical Association Reports.*